ESCAPE
INTO
MEANING

ESCAPE INTO MEANING

ESSAYS ON SUPERMAN, PUBLIC BENCHES, AND OTHER OBSESSIONS

EVAN PUSCHAK

CREATOR OF THE NERDWRITER

ATRIA PAPERBACK

NEW YORK LONDON TORONTO SYDNEY NEW DELHI

An Imprint of Simon & Schuster, Inc.
1230 Avenue of the Americas
New York, NY 10020

First Atria Paperback edition July 2023

ATRIA PAPERBACK and colophon are trademarks of Simon & Schuster, Inc.

For information about special discounts for bulk purchases,
please contact Simon & Schuster Special Sales at 1-866-506-1949 or
business@simonandschuster.com.

The Simon & Schuster Speakers Bureau can bring authors to your live event. For more
information or to book an event, contact the Simon & Schuster Speakers Bureau at
1-866-248-3049 or visit our website at www.simonspeakers.com.

Interior design by Lexy East

Manufactured in U.S.A.

1   3   5   7   9   10   8   6   4   2

Library of Congress Cataloging-in-Publication Data
Names: Puschak, Evan, author.
Title: Escape into meaning : essays on Superman, public benches, and
other obsessions / Evan Puschak.
Description: First Atria Books hardcover edition. | New York : Atria Books, 2022. |
Includes bibliographical references.
Identifiers: LCCN 2021053608 (print) | LCCN 2021053609 (ebook) |
ISBN 9781982163952 (hardcover) | ISBN 9781982163969 (paperback) |
ISBN 9781982163976 (ebook)
Subjects: LCGFT: Essays.
Classification: LCC PS3616.U84 E83 2022 (print) | LCC PS3616.U84 (ebook) |
DDC 814/.6—dc23/eng/20211116
LC record available at https://lccn.loc.gov/2021053608
LC ebook record available at https://lccn.loc.gov/2021053609

ISBN 978-1-9821-6395-2
ISBN 978-1-9821-6396-9 (pbk)
ISBN 978-1-9821-6397-6 (ebook)

For Lissette

One always sees the soul through words.
—Virginia Woolf, from her diary

CONTENTS

ESCAPE
INTO
MEANING

EMERSON'S MAGIC

Growing up in the middle-class Philadelphia suburbs, I always had the impression that education wasn't about education. If you learned something in school, great, but that wasn't the point. The point of school was to get good grades, and the point of good grades was to get into a good college, and the point of a good college was to get a good job, and the point of a good job was some or maybe all of the following: (a) to make money; (b) to be happy; (c) to be independent and not live at home; (d) to seem desirable to potential romantic partners; (e) to not be the type of person your parents are embarrassed by when they're at a dinner party and everyone is talking about their kids. The path splintered after you finally landed a job, but when I was young that seemed a lifetime away. Before then, everything was linear and clearly checkpointed. The critical thing was to cross those checkpoints, and education was just the means to do that, not an end in itself.

At least that's how it felt to me. That's what the messaging in my world sounded like. I heard it from my parents, teachers, tutors, administrators, even students. It wasn't usually explicit. Nobody said my GPA was more important than a familiarity with algebra or American history. That's the kind of cynicism we don't say aloud. But the implication was there, beneath all the lip service paid to "expanding our minds," in the way an A+ was celebrated and rewarded, in the school's ranking of students, in how standardized tests like the SAT boiled you down to a number. As children, we're subject to so much ludicrous authority that we become experts on it. We learn exactly what our world wants from us, so we can appease it and get back to the stuff we really want to do, like *Super Mario Bros. 3*. Did my world want me to know the significance of irony in *Pride and Prejudice*? The atomic structure of various metals? Roman emperors? Not really. It wanted good report cards.

So I obliged. My grades weren't great, but they were good enough, and good enough is all a relatively privileged kid has to be. I did the least amount of work necessary to cross the checkpoints and not be a disappointment to my family. This meant cramming and regurgitating info for tests, instead of actually absorbing knowledge. It meant copying a friend's homework in the hallway before class. It meant reading the CliffsNotes rather than the books. It meant crib sheets hidden in a sleeve or saved on a TI-83 calculator. Why should I have felt any compunction about cheating? My world placed a much greater value on good grades than it did on moral principles. And what's so moral anyway about a system that selects for good test-takers, while leaving plenty of intelligent and talented students behind? No, secondary education didn't feel like education, and high school didn't feel like school. It felt like a recruitment camp, where you had to persuade gatekeeping institutions to award you an opportunity everyone deserves. Ends twisted as that justified whatever means.

This is not to say I had bad teachers or went to bad schools. Some of my teachers were extraordinary, like Mr. Leventhal in eighth-grade English and Mrs. Bienkowski in twelfth-grade economics. They all, I think, sincerely wanted to teach, to pass on knowledge to their students, to help us think critically. (They couldn't have been in it for the money.) But warped systemic incentives can prevail over the good intentions of smart and generous people. Learning is not the chief goal of most American schooling. The chief goal is turning out graduates. And those two things are not the same.

Maybe the system we have now is better than the alternatives. I hope not, but I don't know how to fix it, so I should probably leave the indictments to those who do. All I know is how it made me feel. When I finally crossed the college checkpoint and arrived at Boston University in 2006, a school perfectly "good enough" for my parents, I was a deeply uninspired person, trained to view education as a game, not a source of joy or fulfillment. I enrolled as a film major because I had fun making silly videos with friends. Beyond that, my interests were limited to comic books and . . . that's all.

It was hard to shake that cold and strategic view of learning. At first, I treated college the same as I treated high school, riding the momentum of thinking one way for a dozen years. But after a semester, an aimlessness began to gnaw at me. I still had the job checkpoint ahead, but it didn't motivate with the same fear as earlier ones. In high school, everything matters: tests, papers, homework, participation—all of it contributes to your grade, which contributes to your GPA. If I brought home a C+, I was in deep shit, and my parents were lax compared to some. In college, grades didn't carry the same weight. If I had been studying medicine or law, they would have, but I was a *film major*. No one was going to look at my transcripts ever again. Once I realized that, the Cs opened and rushed forth in great waves. I stopped cramming, stopped buying overpriced textbooks, stopped doing homework. I stopped caring about grades and points and averages.

And I started to learn.

It's amazing how different a class becomes when you're not spending all your time scrawling notes, trying to sort out what will or won't be relevant to some future exam. I recommend it. Take nothing to class but yourself. Listen, ask questions, absorb, have fun. When the test comes, try your best. All you need is a D not to fail out of college. (DISCLAIMER: Do *not* take this course of action if you are studying the aforementioned law or medicine, or have an interest in going to grad school of any kind. Study for the tests, take the notes, have as little fun as possible.)

When I removed the unnecessary stress, I learned how valuable school can be. So many of my professors at BU were *obsessed* with their subjects, and that enthusiasm was infectious. I became fascinated by things that were never even on my radar. Hell, I declared an archaeology minor thanks to one randomly chosen course about the antiquities trade that turned out to be enthralling. If I could go back, I'd cut out most of the film stuff and take a bunch of liberal arts classes instead: history and literature and economics and sociology. Imagine the great professors who passed me by. Imagine the obsessions that could have been . . .

Discovering a love of learning felt like a rebirth. That nagging sense of pointlessness yielded to a promise of substance in every direction. The world lit up with questions, and questions generated questions. It's an exhilarating and terrifying experience to walk the road of your ignorance. Learning, you learn, is not really a process of expanding your mind, but of watching it shrink against all there is to know. It's humbling but addicting. I followed that addiction into a new life, free from GPA anxiety, off the checkpointed path. It made college more enriching, but it went beyond that. Reading no longer felt like a chore. I hopscotched from book to book, chasing enthusiasms that moved faster than I could. I found new passions and complex ideas and finer shades of meaning. Then I found Ralph Waldo Emerson in the Barnes & Noble in Kenmore Square, on the edge of campus, under the CITGO sign.

One afternoon, while skipping a profoundly boring class (they can't all be Archaeology 203), I walked to Kenmore, wandered into the bookstore, and, for no particular reason, picked up a copy of Emerson's essays. I took it to the mini café near the front, bought a coffee and a scone, and read until my life changed its direction, which took about forty minutes.

Reading Emerson was like watching magic. Somehow he was able to retrieve the cloudy, half-formed thoughts in my mind and write them down with astonishing eloquence—a century and a half before I was born! This is the *magic of articulation*, of putting things exactly right, and it's been the basic obsession of all my work since that afternoon in Barnes & Noble.

You know the experience I'm talking about: someone phrases something perfectly and an idea that's been a fog in the background of your mind suddenly solidifies. A lot of the time we aren't fully aware of our thoughts and opinions, so when another person articulates one, it feels strange, like a surprise coming from within. Often it makes us laugh—something all stand-up comedians depend on. Their job is to articulate our opinions in clever ways, to evoke that startling laughter of recognition. The best comedians take the vaguest, most universal musings and sharpen them to a fine point. Emerson does the same.

I bought the book that afternoon—*Essays and Poems* by Ralph Waldo Emerson—but kept coming back to the Barnes & Noble for weeks to read it at the mini café. It became something of a sacred space for me, not because the scones were particularly great, but because it was where I discovered Emerson and was stamped with the joy of that first high. I skipped a good number of classes in that bookstore, and for someone who never played a day of hooky in high school, there was a sense of rebellion in that. Yeah, I know: skipping class to read Emerson is maybe the lamest, least rock-and-roll rebellion in the history of rebellions, but it felt rebellious to me. Caring about something so deeply felt rebellious, and that's the place where Emerson gave me permission to care.*

The more Emerson I read, the more my own thinking seemed murky and confused. The more it seemed like my decisions and beliefs were based on a hodgepodge of old, drifting thought-fragments, corrupted after years without reflection. A paragraph of Emerson's was more complete than my entire belief system. His essays snowballed into towering monuments of self-expression, poetic and staggeringly lucid.

From Emerson, I learned two fundamental truths: first, that *we learn by expressing, not by thinking*, which is to say that knowledge doesn't really exist until you can write it down. What we normally imagine as "thinking" is really just a distracted form of writing, like having a disoriented drunk at a typewriter behind your eyes. Writing sobers him up. The pen (or the word processor) lets the mind compose language into knowledge that's far more sophisticated than what that little boozer can do on his own.

On the spectrum of sophistication, speaking falls somewhere between thinking and writing, but it's the form of language (or thought) construction we use the most. I find that once I articulate something in speech, it sticks in my mind more or less intact—but only for a little while. If it's a thought I want to build on, writing is the only option. Otherwise, it will gradually get pulled into the quicksand of my consciousness, forgotten or folded into a mix of ill-considered motivations.

* I read yesterday that Barnes & Noble shuttered the Kenmore Square branch in 2019, which isn't a great loss, all things considered, but now I know what it feels like to learn that someone demolished your childhood home.

But the mind doesn't need cogent thoughts to operate. That's the second fundamental truth I learned from Emerson, not from his writing directly, but as a consequence of reading it. My brain was getting along just fine in all its hypocrisy and contradiction. If I kept myself busy, I barely noticed the inconsistencies. But once I slowed down and began to wonder who I actually was, what I actually believed—something we're all inclined to do eventually—my tangled self could offer no answers.

So I read more Emerson and found some.

Looking back, I realize he was the perfect thinker for that moment in my life. Escaping from the arid mindset I described above into a jungle of meaning, I needed someone to help me articulate my overwhelming new feelings, to legitimize them for me. Emerson's first essay, "Nature," did exactly that. It's the ideal companion for awakenings.

In the years before its 1836 release, Emerson served as a junior pastor at a Unitarian church in Boston, but quit the ministry after just three years. He'd grown increasingly frustrated with the Church's teaching, believing it to be stale and doctrinaire, so he started to develop his own philosophy. You can hear Emerson's frustrations in the essay's opening lines:

> Our age is retrospective. It builds the sepulchres
> of the fathers. It writes biographies and histories
> and criticism. The foregoing generations beheld
> God and nature face to face; we, through their eyes.
> Why should not we also enjoy an original relation

to the universe? Why should not we have a poetry and philosophy of insight and not of tradition, and a religion by revelation to us, and not the history of theirs?

Is it any wonder this appealed to me? Emerson describes a hollow world of obsolete rules, where scholars squabble over inconsequential details of archaic texts, rather than seek revelations of their own. We shouldn't be guided by tradition just because it's tradition, he says. We shouldn't accept something just because it was written in a book our ancestors deemed sacred. To me, this was high school. It was prioritizing grades over learning. It was the checkpointed path. I, like Emerson, wanted to "enjoy an original relation to the universe." I wanted to discover truths of my own, on my own.

The danger of received wisdom is a fundamental theme of Emerson's early work. In "The American Scholar," he explains how ancient insights get corrupted over time, how "the love of the hero corrupts into the worship of his statue." A book can "become noxious" when it's treated as gospel, when "colleges are built on it" and other books are written about it by those "who set out from accepted dogmas, not from their own sight of principles." This emphasis on old wisdom creates a culture of "bookworms," not thinkers, "meek young men [who] grow up in libraries, believing it their duty to accept the views, which Cicero, which Locke, which Bacon have given, forgetful that Cicero, Locke, and Bacon were only young men in libraries when they wrote these books."

Emerson doesn't discourage the reading of past masters, but he does warn against taking what we read—even from the most respected, *even from him*—on faith. The purpose of books, he says, is to inspire our own ideas, not to demand fealty to theirs. Even genius can be harmful if it over-influences, if I am knocked "clean out of my own orbit, and made a satellite instead of a system." Emerson wants to protect the individual's trust in her own genius, her own capacity to uncover the world's secrets. Books and the institutions that teach them are indispensable tools, but they serve us best "when they aim not to drill, but to create; when they gather from far every ray of various genius to their hospitable halls and, by the concentrated fires, set the hearts of their youth on flame."

Did your schools set you alight? Or did they drill?

Of all institutions, it's the Church that receives Emerson's harshest rebuke, in the famous "Divinity School Address" of 1838. Think of the guts it took to deliver a fiery critique of Christianity to the *Harvard Divinity School*! You have to wonder what the graduating class was thinking, inviting a man, who six years earlier deserted the ministry, to address a fresh crop of new ministers. Emerson condemns the "decaying church" for dwelling with "noxious exaggeration about the person of Jesus," when he is only a man with the same access to the Infinite Soul as everyone else. You can see how denying the special divinity of Jesus might, well, cause a stir.

While some found the speech compelling, many were scandalized by Emerson's radical individualism. It threatened the core of their faith. For Emerson, Jesus was someone who had the courage to seek the infinite in himself, and his example should have been an inspiration for the rest of us to do the same. Instead, Christianity adopted a "vulgar tone of preaching" that commands its followers to "subordinate your nature to Christ's nature," that speaks of "revelation as somewhat long ago given and done, as if God were dead." To Emerson, everything necessary for revelation is available here and now, in nature, in us. God isn't a "vaunting, overpowering, excluding sanctity, but a sweet, natural goodness."

The nice Christians at Harvard can be forgiven for their outrage. This wasn't the Christianity they knew. It was a different philosophy altogether, incompatible with their beliefs, bordering on atheism.

Despite accusations, Emerson was not a nonbeliever— but I am, and in "The Divinity School Address" I saw ideas that made more sense to me than anything I heard in synagogue as a kid. It affirmed the essential beauty of all things, a harmony between humanity and nature. You don't need faith to feel a oneness with the universe. Emerson, it seemed to me, emphasized the vital things about spirituality, while discarding all its outworn trappings.

But it wasn't just that he emphasized values that resonated with me, it was *how* he emphasized them. When Emerson writes that "every man's condition is a solution in hieroglyphic to the inquiries he would put," he captures for me the essence of introspection. Reading that line in "Nature" launched a lifetime of reflection. And when I read the following passage, from "The American

Scholar," I found the confidence to express what reflection taught me:

> In going down into the secrets of his own mind, [a person] has descended into the secrets of all minds. . . . The poet, in utter solitude remembering his spontaneous thoughts and recording them, is found to have recorded that which men in cities vast find true for them also. . . . The deeper he dives into his privatest, secretest presentiment, to his wonder he finds this is the most acceptable, most public and universally true.

I knew Emerson was right about this because that's what he was doing for me. I felt exactly how he felt when he read Montaigne's essays:

> A single odd volume of Cotton's translation of the Essays remained to me from my father's library, when a boy. It lay long neglected, until, after many years, when I was newly escaped from college, I read the book, and procured the remaining volumes. I remember the delight and wonder in which I lived with it. It seemed to me as if I had myself written the book, in some former life, so sincerely it spoke to my thought and experience.

It was doubly astounding to read this when I'd already had the feeling, as I said above, that Emerson was somehow articulating my own thoughts.

He articulated *that* thought, too!

If Emerson was mentioned in one of my high school classes, I must've been daydreaming (which was my default mode) because I don't remember it. That, or I brushed him off as a dreary old statue of a man, who, from his high perch in the American Pantheon, had little to say to someone like me. Clearly, I was an idiot. If there's anything Emerson is not, it's dreary. He's a thinker bursting with ecstasy for life, and his prose is an attempt to bottle that ecstasy. He approaches everything with a child's sensitivity. Often the essays swell with excitement, like a nine-year-old itching to tell you the *coolest thing ever*:

> What angels invented these splendid ornaments, these rich conveniences, this ocean of air above, this ocean of water beneath, this firmament of earth between? this zodiac of lights, this tent of dropping clouds, this striped coat of climates, this fourfold year?

Emerson is the most eloquent nine-year-old in history. And like a nine-year-old, he's never jaded. He's here for the drowsy and jaded souls of 1836 or today, to shake us out of it: "If the stars should appear one night in a thousand years, how would men believe and adore; and preserve for many generations the remembrance of the city of God which had been shown!"

He's also here to renew our self-confidence. That's the crux of what is likely his most famous essay, "Self-Reliance," a fullhearted plea for the individual to "Trust thyself." If his earlier essays touched on the theme, this one places it at the core of his philosophy. Emerson rails against conformity as an epidemic evil: "Whoso would be a man must be a nonconformist," he says. "Nothing is at last sacred but the integrity of your own mind." We should refuse to "capitulate to badges and names, to large societies and dead institutions," then prepare for a backlash to that refusal: "For nonconformity the world whips you with its displeasure." You have only to glance at Twitter to see a confirmation of this. But we need not worry, says Emerson, for "the sour faces of the multitude, like their sweet faces, have no deep cause, but are put on and off as the wind blows and the newspaper directs." What we should really worry about is becoming part of that multitude, of choosing compliance over intuition, of imitating.

In the years since I first read this essay, I've come to see the limits of Emerson's gospel of the self. In an admirable polemic against conformity, he goes too far in the other direction, sometimes crossing the line that separates healthy self-esteem from egomania. Trusting your gut is one thing; trusting it against all else is another. Sometimes it can be hard to make out when Emerson's being literal and when he's using hyperbole as a rhetorical device. Either way, saying "the only right is what is after my constitution, the only wrong what is against it" is excessive.

Intuition often fails us, especially when coupled with ignorance, or when we take our experience to be representative of *all* experience. While I do believe that in many cases, the deeper we descend into our own minds, the more universal it gets, I also know that is *not* true in many cases. And if there's anything the revolutions in social justice have taught me, it's that our own privileges can block us from seeing the truth of others' lives. There is no basement level in my consciousness that could have clued me in to my wife, Lissette's, experience as a Mexican American, for example. The solution to that cluelessness is not more reflection, but to ask questions and listen.

At times, Emerson's contempt for society's conforming pressures slips into a distrust of society itself: "Society never advances," he declares. "It recedes as fast on one side as it gains on another." Between individuals and the collective, Emerson favors the individual—to a fault. Society *does* advance, and only when people stand together, when they act collectively. Emerson's self-reliance reads as self-absorption in certain passages, and self-absorption being the keynote of our culture for some decades now, it's clear how such thinking can hinder progress and cause all kinds of disastrous inequality. Not all multitudes are bad.

I don't agree with everything Emerson wrote. If I did, Emerson himself would be the first to disapprove. But his points, in "Self-Reliance" and elsewhere, are subtle enough to overcome their excesses and still be of great value to the modern reader. There are ways Emerson's exaltation of the self goes too far, but it's also an essential message, made all the more essential for the beauty of its articulation. We all need to forge a confidence in our own mind. To achieve great things, we first need to believe we're *capable* of great things. That belief, as we know, wavers. It erodes against a constant bombardment of self-doubt. If you're feeling low, "Self-Reliance" is the best pep talk imaginable: "You cannot hope too much or dare too much. There is at this moment for you an utterance brave and grand as the colossal chisel of Phidias, or the trowel of the Egyptians, or the pen of Moses, or Dante, but different from all these." And confidence in the self, once attained, gives you the confidence to see its shortcomings.

At nineteen, I needed more than confidence; I needed permission to break free from the only value system I'd ever known, a value system shared by so many in my social universe. This isn't uncommon, of course. I was probably the billionth eighteen-year-old to feel that way, the billionth bewildered teenager who left home for school, only to be shocked that the wider world didn't operate the same way as Anytown, USA. But being the billionth didn't make it any easier to step off the checkpointed path, to swim against the current—even if that current was nothing but a lazy river compared to what others have to face. I tacked this passage to my bedroom wall:

> O father, O mother, O wife, O brother, O friend,
> I have lived with you after appearances hitherto.
> Henceforward I am the truth's . . . I appeal from your
> customs. I must be myself. I cannot break myself any
> longer for you, or you. If you can love me for what
> I am, we shall be the happier. If you cannot, I will
> still seek to deserve that you should. I won't hide my
> tastes or aversions. I will so trust that what is deep is
> holy, that I will do strongly before the sun and moon
> whatever inly rejoices me, and the heart appoints.

Overdramatic? Sure. Though it would've been far more dramatic if I followed through with my plan to mail the quote to my parents. A lingering fear of embarrassment stopped me, but it didn't stop me from making several other Emerson-style declarations during that period, which I cringe to remember now. At the time, however, I needed Emerson's drama, his fearless, poetic conviction. I was a self-conscious kid, always anxious about what others thought of me. In Emerson, I saw someone unafraid of naked sincerity, willing to brave the severe light of judgment to express himself with the fire he had within. Maybe his self-assurance helped him to feel less vulnerable. Maybe he felt as vulnerable as I did, but spoke his truth nonetheless, believing it to be more valuable than a life without embarrassment. I'm just as self-conscious now as then, but Emerson gave me the nerve to overrule that annoying impulse.

That's what I'm doing now.

In these four essays—"Nature," "The American Scholar," "The Divinity School Address," and "Self-Reliance"— Emerson lays out his special brand of transcendentalism. It has a few ruling themes, but his philosophy is not systematic. It doesn't have the internal consistency of, say, Immanuel Kant's work, or John Stuart Mill's, one of his contemporaries. It can't be structured into a dogma of its own. Emerson wasn't that rigorous, and he didn't aim to be. As he says in one of his most famous lines, from "Self-Reliance": "A foolish consistency is the hobgoblin of little minds, adored by little statesmen and philosophers and divines." Some see this inconsistency, this fluidity, as a weakness of Emerson's work; others point to it as the best reason for his longevity. You can put me in the second camp.

There's obviously a place for philosophical systems, but what makes them rigorous also makes them rigid. A flaw threatens the whole structure. Emerson's writing is never so fragile. It doesn't resemble a building so much as a great winding river: jump in at any point from the source to the sea and you'll be propelled with great speed through flourishing terrain, awestruck by iridescent flora you've never seen before, passing one after the next. As you age, the course of the river changes. What was dry now floods the banks. What was straight now bends and curves. Even after decades, there is always more to see.

Emerson isn't a philosopher in the pure sense or a theologian. He's an intellectual adventurer, a journalist of the mind, an *essayist*. When you move beyond the core transcendental pieces, you get a better sense of this range. He tackles everything from love to manners, history to illusion, friendship to politics. None of these has the cachet of "Nature" or "Self-Reliance," but many, in my opinion, are stronger. They dance across the boundary between art and argument, poetry and prose. They make you question the point of those distinctions.

Take, for example, "Experience," which attempts to describe the feeling of being alive. What predominates, in this often pessimistic essay, is a sense of confusion, and he begins by dropping us into that feeling:

> We wake and find ourselves on a stair; there are stairs below us, which we seem to have ascended; there are stairs above us, many a one, which go upward and out of sight. But the genius which according to the old belief stands at the door by which we enter, and gives us the Lethe to drink, that we may tell no tales,

mixed the cup too strongly, and we can't shake off the
lethargy now at noonday. Sleep lingers all our lifetime
about our eyes, as night hovers all day in the boughs
of the fir-tree. All things swim and glitter.

This passage is as dreamlike and immersive as a short film
by David Lynch. It captures that occasional experience we
all have of *waking up into our own lives*, not quite knowing how we got here or where we're going. The essay is
about the difficulty of attaining an accurate perspective on
life while it's happening, about the ways our mind warps
experience—so Emerson warps the reading experience in
turn. "All things swim and glitter," including his prose:

Dream delivers us to dream, and there is no end
to illusion. Life is a train of moods like a string of
beads, and, as we pass through them, they prove to
be many colored lenses which paint the world their
own hue, and each shows only what lies in its focus.

And so each new paragraph adopts a different mood, al-
tering his perspective on perspective. He's hopeful, then
cynical. Assured, then full of doubt, then melancholy, then
baffled. The result is an essay that simulates the psychological swings it's analyzing.

If there's a vein of sorrow in "Experience," that's because
Emerson wrote it shortly after the death of his five-year-
old son, Waldo, who succumbed to scarlet fever in 1842.
One way you can read this essay is as a processing of that
grief, which manifested in ways Emerson didn't expect:

In the death of my son, now more than two years ago, I seem to have lost a beautiful estate—no more. I cannot get it nearer to me. If tomorrow I should be informed of the bankruptcy of my principal debtors, the loss of property would be a great inconvenience to me, perhaps, for many years; but it would leave me as it found me—neither better nor worse. So it is with this calamity: it does not touch me: some thing which I fancied was a part of me, which could not be torn away without tearing me, nor enlarged without enriching me, falls from me and leaves no scar. It was caducous. I grieve that grief can teach me nothing, nor carry me one step into real nature.

I haven't endured such a loss, but in these words I feel the bitter apathy of Emerson's heart. Experience should teach us something. Wisdom should be the compensation for failure and loss: "To know a little, would be worth the expense of this world." But this grief is empty. The only thing it can teach is that it doesn't, which is the coldest comfort. "The dearest events are summer rain," he declares, "and we the Para coats that shed every drop."

After opening with confusion and tragedy, Emerson goes on to explore the things that mediate our experience of reality. Mood is one, the "many colored lenses" that distort what we see. Another is temperament, some blend of genetics and environment that shapes our choices and "shuts us in a prison we cannot see":

There is an optical illusion about every person we meet. In truth, they are all creatures of a given temperament, which will appear in a given character, whose boundaries they will never pass: but we look at them, they seem alive and we presume there is impulse in them. In the moment it seems impulse; in the year, in the lifetime, it turns out to be a certain uniform tune which the revolving barrel of the music-box must play.

Have you had the experience of finding yourself back in the same place again and again, after attempts to start over, with new friends, new partners? Maybe you believed you were finally changing; then, looking back, you hear that "certain uniform tune," your temperament finding its way to the surface once again. Does this square with the assured tone of "Self-Reliance"? It's the opposite of a pep talk, if anything. Emerson evokes these insecurities as only he can, with alarming clarity, mustering the same persuasive force for self-doubt that he did for self-confidence.

There are moments in "Experience" when Emerson seems resigned to personality determinism. And there are moments when he fears there is no way to know the world outside his mind. But then there are passages where he rejects ignorance and despair. In a swell of optimism, Emerson denies the idea that "given such an embryo, such a history must follow," because it overlooks our capacity for *creativity*, the door in our mind that never closes: "At one whisper of these high powers, we awake from ineffectual struggles with this nightmare." Here again, the essay demonstrates its own point.

Like all of his work, "Experience" contains countless jewels of insight, quotes you could tack on a bedroom wall. But what really makes the essay extraordinary is how it struggles with itself. On the sentence level, Emerson is peerless. But here is a subtler form of articulation, suited to the subtlety of the subject. Rather than trying to make a straightforward argument about the distortions of the mind with a distorted mind, Emerson *exhibits* his psyche for the reader, conflicts and all. He lets his confidence and his doubt have it out on the page. Tone challenges text. Paragraph complicates paragraph. Any attempt to explain the texture of human experience is certain to be flawed, so Emerson creates that texture instead. We exit the essay as dazed as we entered it, but with a nuanced appreciation of his mind—and ours.

Essay by essay, Emerson brought my life into focus. I was entranced, enlightened, and inspired. I couldn't believe someone knew how to do these kinds of things with language. It was magic, and I wanted to learn it. I wanted to retrieve the cloudy, half-formed thoughts from my head and give them shape, make them real. I wanted to excavate the secrets of my mind and see if others recognized them. I wanted to know what I actually believed, and to do that I had to write. So I wrote, and it was godawful.

But after a while, it was less godawful. And then only a little godawful. Then I graduated from godawful to awful, then from awful to bad, then from bad to unremarkable. I'm still climbing that stair, a long way from Emerson, but a long way from where I started. In the process, I read much more than just these essays, of course. Literature overflows with magicians of articulation, from Homer to Shakespeare to Toni Morrison. Each has their own tricks, their own subject matter, but all have the same goal: to say something true, to find "a thought so passionate and alive, that, like the spirit of a plant or an animal, it has an architecture of its own, and adorns nature with a new thing."

It turns out that the books I was assigned in high school *are* brilliant. It turns out the irony in *Pride and Prejudice* really *is* significant. In school, I saw that book as a hurdle, one of many on the long path from ninth-grade English to some nebulous future job. Its content wasn't important in itself, only as a means to answer test questions, just like the test was a means to maintain a GPA, like the GPA was a ticket to college, etc. When I picked up the book again, I read it with new eyes, the eyes Emerson gave me, and sure enough, it expanded my mind, just like my teachers hoped it would. Unclouded by dry pragmatism, this second education was better than the first. I learned for learning's sake, for joy, for no reason at all. Ironically, this goalless self-schooling proved far more useful than the system that prioritized *use* above all.

"I was simmering, simmering, simmering," Walt Whitman once told a friend. "Emerson brought me to a boil."

When Emerson found me, I was barely lukewarm, but the result was the same. Everything I've written since that afternoon in Kenmore, including this book, I owe to his inspiration. "The man is only half himself," he writes in "The Poet," "the other half is his expression." More than a decade ago, Emerson helped me with the first part. The second is his work in progress.

I THINK THE INTERNET WANTS TO BE MY MIND

Where do we find ourselves? On a timeline of which we cannot see the ends, and believe it has none. We wake and find ourselves on a TikTok; there are TikToks above us, which we seem to have watched; there are TikToks below us, many a one, which go downward and out of sight. But the company that stands at the door by which we enter, and gives us the algorithm to browse, that we may want to stay longer, wrote the code too strongly, and we cannot get off the platform now at midnight. Posts linger all our lifetime about our eyes, as night hovers all day in the boughs of the fir tree. All things Instagram and Twitter. Our life is not so much threatened as our perception. Ghostlike we glide through nature, and should not know our place IRL again.

Every Sunday at nine a.m., my iPhone sends me a message. It's the Weekly Screen Time Report, and the news is never good. "Your screen time was up 6 percent last week," iPhone says with a tone of disappointment, "for an average of 5 hours and 49 minutes a day." Usually I'm using the phone when this notification appears, which only adds insult to injury. (Or does iPhone wait for me to use it, to guarantee maximum self-loathing?) Few things are more dispiriting than receiving that alert when you're on the toilet watching Will Smith solve a Rubik's Cube.

Immediately I start doing math: 24 hours minus 8 hours of sleep equals 16 hours of waking life each day. 5 hours, 49 minutes, divided by 16 equals 0.36, which means I spend *over a third* of my waking life gazing at this phone screen. Add that to computer time and TV time and the percentages are too massive to bear. A wave of regret passes over me. Fortunately, the perfect tool for repressing unhappy feelings is in my hands:

Will completes the Cube in . . . fifty-five seconds!

Maybe Apple's screen time management tools work for some people, but they don't work for me. By "work," I mean curtail usage and promote self-restraint. A steadily growing average proves the opposite effect: usage is up, restraint is nonexistent. If I had any restraint, YouTube wouldn't keep serving me videos I've already watched a dozen times. I can almost hear the algorithm chuckling when it tosses that clip of Michael Jordan and Charles Barkley on *Oprah* into the Recommended sidebar. It baits me like the best fisherman, and I go for it like the trout that I am. Another twenty-four minutes added to the weekly report. When I see the hours added up, I feel shame, which is what iPhone wants me to feel, but that's a flawed motivator. Too much shame and the system shuts down, burying the emotion instead of addressing its cause.

There's something very wrong about the iPhone being a policeman of its own use. Apple builds the shiniest, most addictive and useful tool in human history, then installs an app that's supposed to help us use it *less*? That's like McDonald's serving Big Macs with a note that reads: "Eat only 30 percent of this Big Mac, as a whole Big Mac is not good for you." If that's true, maybe don't engineer your burgers to be 100 percent addictive. Maybe don't build a device that's designed to boost dependency, then, on that same device, piously offer us a bit of software to break that dependency. Tools like that are hair dryers against a hurricane. The modern world is built to obliterate restraint, and technology enthusiastically leads the charge.

Screen time management tools are little more than PR stunts, from another industry promoting solutions to problems it creates. Tobacco giants did (and do) the same; so do oil companies. In 2005, British Petroleum popularized the term "carbon footprint" to divert the public's attention away from BP's role in climate change and toward individual responsibility. You can still use their "carbon footprint calculator" to shame yourself. "The first step to reducing your emissions is to know where you stand," BP tweeted in 2019, with a link to the calculator. It's nauseating. The Weekly Screen Time Report attempts the same shift in focus—away from tech companies, toward you. Of course, individuals bear responsibility for their own harmful addictions, to cigarettes or oil or greenhouse gases, but the creators of these things are culpable as well, and PR posturing only tries to obscure that.

But the fact that Apple feels the need to posture tells us something. It testifies to the reality of the problem. Companies don't voluntarily admit to the damage they cause.

That's bad business. They would much rather refuse to acknowledge that damage, or deny it, or sponsor "academic" research to "prove" there is in fact no damage at all. If a corporation is conceding to harm—even if it's reluctant, partial, and only a posture—it means the outcry against that harm has reached a critical volume. It means isolated complaints have graduated to widespread distress, which is finally impossible to ignore or deny.

If screen addiction weren't a real problem, could you imagine Apple CEO Tim Cook, or any CEO, saying something like this: "We do not want people using our products too much." That is an actual thing Cook said on the *Outside* podcast in 2020, talking about his experience with the Screen Time app. "Screen Time was a way of making all of us aware of how much time we're spending in our technology." Note the similarity to BP's carbon footprint language: *us, we're, our.* Cook goes on: "I started asking myself: Why do I need all these notifications? Why do I really need this? Do I really need to understand things in the moment they're happening? I started taking a meat-ax out to some of these things that would grab my attention but didn't need to in the moment." Cook maintains that "we never designed our products to dominate people's lives." If that's the case, why do you need a fucking meat-ax?

Clearly, Apple's read the room. They're actively staking out a position as the "responsible" tech giant on device addiction, selflessly encouraging us to put their beautiful products down for a spell. As Cook says, "We've never been into this 'How long is somebody spending on our property and let's try to figure out a way to make that as high as possible.'" Cook's defense doubles as an attack: he applauds Apple, while condemning its Big Tech competitors for their roles in the attention economy.

Fortunately for Apple, it has the perfect foils in Facebook, Google, Netflix, Twitter, and TikTok (all of which you can easily install on your iPhone). Maybe the iPhone is hard to put down, but it's nothing compared to the infinite scroll of Facebook's News Feed, algorithmically designed to trap you in a self-reinforcing, outrage-inducing bubble while it extracts your personal data to serve you targeted ads. That's the heated subtext of Cook's remarks.

He's not wrong. When it comes to the damaging effects of today's tech, Apple is probably not the worst offender. Apple's revenue comes largely from product purchases. Facebook and Twitter and TikTok and Google offer free services to customers, then give sophisticated marketing tools to advertisers that allow them to target segments of their vast user bases. In the third quarter of 2020, Facebook posted $21.5 billion in revenue, of which $21.2 billion was advertising revenue, or *98.6 percent*!

As many others have pointed out, this means that advertisers are Facebook's real customers. Users are its product. Because of this, Facebook and other internet services that rely on advertising revenue are incentivized to keep you in their ecosystems for as long as possible. The more you engage—like, post, comment, click, scroll, subscribe—the more you reveal about your preferences. The more you reveal about your preferences, the easier it is to predict what you might like to buy, the easier it is to modify your behavior to compel you to buy.

This ad-based system is the source of most of the harmful effects we commonly associate with modern tech: screen addiction, fake news, lack of privacy, mental health issues, and political polarization. I'm not breaking news here. These issues are at the forefront of public discourse, litigated constantly in both traditional and social media. But you don't need to read about these problems to know they exist. You know they exist because, like the rest of us, you experience them as part of your daily life. You see the fake news, lament the polarization, get spooked when Google serves you an ad for something you were chatting to a friend about yesterday. You feel the pull of that glowing rectangle on your nightstand, the first thing you grab in the morning, the last thing you touch at night. You've been finding it hard to concentrate lately, reading the same book for months, unable to make progress. You feel more anxious and envious and afraid. You're lonelier. Spread thin. Not in control.

Or maybe I'm just projecting.

None of us needs more research to verify something we feel all the time. At a Senate hearing in 2020, Facebook CEO Mark Zuckerberg testified that he didn't "think the research has been conclusive" on whether social media is addictive. Despite the fact that there is plenty of good research finding that it is (and that social media addiction correlates positively with serious mental health problems like depression), I don't need an academic paper to tell me what's happening inside my head. I've got proof coming out the wazoo. When my laptop is taking a second to buffer a YouTube video and I grab my phone to scroll Facebook rather than wait—that's my proof. When I walk face-first into a doorframe because I'm reading tweets—that's my proof. When I go to pee but miss the toilet bowl because I'm watching TikTok stars synchronize dance to BENEE's "Supalonely"— that's my (humiliating) proof.

I can't recall a single day in the last decade in which I didn't access the internet. More and more, that access is enabled by my phone and mediated by social media, its algorithms and machine learning, its profit motive. Five hours and forty-nine minutes a day may seem like a lot, but to me that number feels low. When I lie down to bed each night, putting my phone, aptly, on Do Not Disturb, I have a hard time remembering ten unbroken minutes in the day during which I did not, in some way, connect. The internet permeates my waking life. It's omnipresent, invasive. Part of me lives online now. That's indisputable. But lately I've begun to wonder about the opposite: *How much of the internet lives in me?*

Here's an example of what I mean:

When the *Cats* movie trailer landed on YouTube in July 2019, I did not watch it with my eyes, but with the eyes of Twitter—the eyes of the internet. The trailer flaunted its hellish imagery of human/cat hybrids dancing along neon-lit Victorian streets, and yes, it alarmed me but only superficially; my mind was too busy categorizing the public reaction.

We were going to have a field day with this. First there would be tweets, then articles, then articles compiling the tweets. At least one headline would have "uh-oh" in it, reporters would jostle for the best feline pun, somebody would vow to scratch their eyes out. Memes, I was sure, were already flooding the feeds. They'd start with captioned screenshots, then develop into more complex forms. Perhaps one or two would live on after the dust settled and be applied to future events. The broad strokes of the coming twenty-four hours were evident to me; the specifics would be a surprise, as they always were, more creative than I could imagine or invent.

Fourteen hours after its premiere, the trailer's dislikes outnumbered likes by about 14,000 (47,000 to 33,000). That would probably get worse as the day rolled on. Commenters criticized, but without the bitterness a ratio like that usually indicates. The top comment on YouTube, from blueberrycharm, quoted a popular line from *Spy Kids 2*: "Do you think God stays in heaven because he too lives in fear of what he's created?" Mostly people made jokes like that; some were shocked, some appalled, some were speechless and said so. But almost none seemed personally insulted. Not even Tim Hawley, another commenter, who declared that "there aren't enough words in the English language to describe the awful sensation my body is feeling after watching this atrocious abomination." In comments-section vernacular, that read to me as mild annoyance.

To understand the online reaction to the *Cats* trailer, I drew on similar incidents from the past. Believe it or not, *Cats* was the *third* movie of 2019 to feature deeply troubling CGI characters. In February, Disney dropped the first trailer for *Aladdin*, revealing Will Smith as a disproportioned blue humanoid, somehow chubby *and* shredded: Genie, allegedly. "My man Will Smith be looking like a deformed teletubbie," commented BigBag. The reaction was harsh: Smith was clowned for days and the film became a token of Disney's rapacious drive to live-action-ize everything in its repertoire. "Our 3 Wishes Are All for Will Smith's Genie in 'Aladdin' to Go Away," *Vice* opined.

The second episode was worse. In April, Paramount released its *Sonic the Hedgehog* trailer, and when audiences saw that the filmmakers overhauled Sonic's physique to give him a more human shape, they erupted. The criticism was so loud Paramount agreed to a redesign of the character. "Thank you for the support. And the criticism," tweeted director Jeff Fowler. "The message is loud and clear . . . you aren't happy with the design & you want changes. It's going to happen." It's a move that cost Paramount millions, while logging millions of views for YouTubers who made fun of the trailer in ever more creative ways.

I didn't think the *Cats* trailer would get the same backlash as *Sonic* or *Aladdin*, but they were important analogues. All these things—the dislike-to-like ratio, the comments, the tweets, the articles, the examples of *Sonic* and *Aladdin*—were reference points. They helped me understand what the internet thought, and what the internet would like me to think.

I googled "cats" to confirm my sense of the situation.

"I don't know why you're all freaking out over miniature yet huge cats with human celebrity faces and sexy breasts performing a demented dream ballet for kids," tweeted Louis Virtel.

Next, the Top Stories side-scroll: "The 'Cats' trailer is here and it's horrifying the internet," reported CNN. These days, you find a lot of headlines referring to "the internet" as a monolith, a collective mind. It's the same with Twitter. Twitter thinks, Twitter rages, Twitter is sad, confused, gives condolences.

Boston Globe: "Cats" Trailer Unites Internet in
Abject Terror

The Week: Downright Nightmarish *Cats* Trailer
Stuns Critics: "My Eyes Are Bleeding"
A.V. Club: Your Eyeballs Are Not Ready for the
Horrors Within the *Cats* Trailer
The Atlantic: I Watched the *Cats* Trailer, and I
Have Some Questions
BuzzFeed: Here Are the Funniest Tweets About
the New *Cats* Trailer
Salon: Why Do the Cats in "Cats" Look Like
Medieval Art Gone Wrong? And Other Burning
Questions
Elle: The Five Stages of Dealing with the "Cats"
Trailer
Wired: A Feline Anatomy Expert Weighs In on
That *Cats* Trailer

Some headlines were creative, most recycled old language; together they broadcast a subtle opinion about the situation. It was relieving that this opinion matched my expectation— though I should've guessed that people were going to swap the trailer audio for music from actual horror movies. Arguably the most popular thing to come out of the first day of *Cats* commentary was Ian Abramson's mashup of *Cats* with the song from Jordan Peele's *Us* trailer. The unsettling remix of "I Got 5 On It" by Luniz fit like a glove. The next day *BuzzFeed* caught up with Abramson to discuss. "When something like this happens on the internet it feels like a gift," Abramson said. "That we can get something so completely batshit crazy that wasn't trying to be." *BuzzFeed* reports that the L.A.-based comedian "noticed people comparing the film online to a horror movie" when he came up with the idea. Abramson saw what we wanted, and he spoke for us.

> *A.V. Club*: This *Cats/Us* Trailer Mashup Is
> Hideously Purrfect
> *Insider*: Someone Put the Creepy Music from
> "Us" over the New "Cats" Trailer and People
> Think It's Much More Fitting

Then Jordan Peele quote-tweeted Abramson, adding: "Yes."

> *Entertainment Weekly*: Jordan Peele Agrees:
> *Cats* Trailer Fits Better with the Song from *Us*

What I read helped me understand what we thought. The vitriol was pretty light, as I imagined it would be. In fact, even before the close of the first day a countermovement of support had begun to form. "The *Cats* movie-musical trailer looks great," *Slate*'s Marissa Martinelli wrote, "whatever the haters say." NBC News's Maura Johnston was won over by Jennifer Hudson's rendition of "Memory," the show's biggest tune. She "got the sort of chill that only a tour de force performance of classic Broadway schmaltz could." Theater fans, it seems to me, are more forgiving than society at large, especially for eccentric displays of sentimentality. Would they adopt this misfit project as their own?

Others predicted box office success, despite the VFX snafu. Scott Mendelson from *Forbes* was the first to advance this view: " 'Cats': With a Purrfectly Bonkers Trailer, Universal Has No Claws for Alarm." Despite social media's mocking, Mendelson believed *Cats* was "positioning itself as the big musical of Christmas 2019, which means it will likely print enough money to fill all the world's litter boxes and then some." He drew on the track record of recent musical hits, like Tom Hooper's earlier film *Les Misérables*, which grossed $422 million worldwide, and 2017's *The Greatest Show-man*, which did abysmally on opening weekend, only to slow-burn to over $430 million (plus much more from its wildly popular soundtrack). Theater geeks tilt scales.

With all that info, I was able to categorize our reaction to the *Cats* trailer alongside similar reactions to *Sonic the Hedgehog* and *Aladdin*, but with subtle variations due to its proximity to theater culture. As time went on, I'd be able to refine that judgment. The internet's feelings are complex, but not infinitely varied. The more you consume the flows of tweets, videos, articles, comments, the easier it gets to bracket that complexity and understand its outer limits. And when you understand what the internet thinks, you understand what it's okay to say. And when you understand what it's okay to say, you can add your part to the symphony, you can collect your likes, you can smother incompatible views.

Or you can just watch.

And let the internet flow through you.

And let the internet *become* you.

I wrote the above a day after the *Cats* trailer came out, attempting to recount my thinking in the hour after I watched it. I wondered then, and still wonder: Was it really *my* thinking? Or was the internet thinking through me?

Of course, this is a ridiculous example. I spent an hour of my life absorbing the discourse around *the fucking* Cats *trailer*. Is there anything more fleeting, more insignificant, than that? I doubt it. But when I look back on my internet consumption, I'm forced to admit that a shamefully big part of it is comprised of five-minute or ten-minute or hour-long chunks devoted to fleeting and insignificant things. Maybe you know what I mean.

We all understand that the internet excels at capturing attention: alerts, notifications, clickbait, the Recommended tabs, the automatic next episode. But what happens to our attention once its captured? Are we really *engaging* with the content we're served? Do we exist at all in these rabbit holes and time sucks? Increasingly, it feels less like I'm using my mind online, and more like my mind is being used, channeled, like I'm a medium for some vast, foreign spirit. What I wrote in 2019, that hour after the *Cats* trailer, reads like the record of an absurd séance.

I am not there at all.

To the internet, I'm just another device. My mind plays the content it supplies me, and when that content plays, I disappear. So much web surfing is passive. Even things that are technically active (scrolling, clicking, liking, searching) take on a passive quality. Ever involuntarily open a new tab and type "Facebook" into the search bar? Sometimes I notice three tabs of the *New York Times* open, and wonder when I did that, how I did it without realizing.

Even as I followed the thread of *Cats* commentary—checking tweets, reading headlines, cross-referencing videos, seeking a consensus—it felt like viewing, not doing, like floating downstream. If I raised up out of myself, I would have seen a hunched body with glazed eyes, reflecting a

scrolling news feed. It's an image out of science fiction. It's
The Matrix, those people in their pods of pink goo, hooked
up by wires to power stations where machines harvest their
body heat for energy. Only there are no wires in our version,
and the machines are controlled (for now) by profit-seek-
ing humans, and they don't want our heat. They want our
attention and money.

Not all content consumption is passive. Good books,
films, journalism, videos, podcasts, etc., encourage you to
think critically. When you've finished a book or an album,
there should be a period of time for you to reflect on what
you've experienced. You should have a break to let your
mind wander, to examine your response, to write your
thoughts down, to discuss them with others. That's one
reason I love seeing movies at the theater. We talk about
preserving the communal experience of watching movies, but what about when the movie ends, that ritual of
slowly getting up, emerging into the lobby, and waiting
until someone finally says, "So what did you think?" The
conversation that follows, in the car ride home or over
drinks at a bar, is what makes the passive viewing experience active.

The internet isn't interested in those gaps, those moments of reflection or conversation. It wants all your moments. As soon as you're done with one thing, it brings you
without delay to the next. Even as you're watching something, the user interface lays out a menu of possible next
things in a sidebar, so it can siphon off a little of your focus.
Or it just plays that thing automatically. Netflix's Autoplay
is the equivalent of putting a six-pack on an alcoholic's

kitchen counter. You *could* stop yourself, but they're making it so easy not to. The modern world obliterates restraint. The internet obliterates the time between experiences.

Netflix CEO Reed Hastings tipped his hand to this idea in 2017, declaring "we are really competing with sleep on the margin." Every minute of waking life, he assumes, is conquerable. The final frontier are those eight hours of slumber. Why does it have to be eight? Surely, Netflix can carve off one or two for itself. "You get a show or a movie you're really dying to watch and you end up staying up late at night," Hastings told Summit LA17, "so we actually compete with sleep—and we're winning!" Those of us who routinely binge into the wee hours agree.

With breaks between things erased, web surfing becomes a different experience than other forms of media consumption. It's passive, but it's also *self-dissolving*. The subject doing the surfing is replaced temporarily by the internet's programmed rhythms. When you glance at the clock to see two hours have evaporated, this, I believe, is what happened. As for *why* it happens, I think that has to do with how the human mind functions.

When I was an undergrad at Boston University, I studied with Liah Greenfeld, a sociology professor and renowned historian of nationalism. She was one of a handful of teachers in my life who really had an impact on me, who helped me to look at the world in fresh ways. When I took her course in 2010, she was nearing the completion of an ambitious book about mental illness, called *Mind, Modernity, Madness: The Impact of Culture on Human Experience*. In class, we read the manuscript together, then discussed in detail her theories and arguments. She used us as whetstones, inviting us to challenge any idea in an effort to make the book sharper. It was my final year of schooling, but the first time I felt like I was actually contributing to something.

In 2013, Professor Greenfeld published *Mind, Modernity, Madness* to acclaim. I recommend it, even if you aren't interested in mental health. It's painstakingly researched but incredibly readable, and her theory of mental illness is derived from more fundamental theories of culture and the mind, which have all kinds of interesting applications to other fields. In fact, that was our final assignment: to apply Professor Greenfeld's theories to a subject of our choosing. At the time, suffering from senioritis, I didn't make much of an effort, handing in a lackluster paper on god knows what. But the ideas stuck in my head, and I think her theory of mind, specifically, is useful for understanding the role of the internet in our lives.

Maybe she'll consider amending my grade.

For Greenfeld, *the brain* and *the mind* are different things—connected but not the same. Almost all animals have brains. They collect information from the senses, then coordinate activity based on that info. Brains enable a being to read *signs*. The environment is constantly *sign*ifying to the animal brain, and the animal reacts with behaviors coded into their DNA by thousands of years of evolution. "A whiff of odor signifies the presence of a prowling lioness or leopard to the gazelle," writes Greenfeld. "It utters a cry which signifies it to others in the herd, they spring into flight."

Being animals ourselves, the world signifies to us, too, and we can read signs with the best of our animal cousins. But the mental life of humans is exponentially more complex than that of even the smartest nonhuman animals—as a result, we became the dominant species on Earth. What accounts for this difference? Is it the size of our brains? Greenfeld doesn't think so. Human consciousness is unique, she argues, because it exists not only within the reality of signs, but also within the reality of *symbols*.

Signs correspond to stimuli in the world and pre-determined behaviors. When the gazelle smells the leopard, it has no choice but to run. The sign triggers the reaction. The meanings of symbols, on the other hand, are invented, intentional, and get their significance from the *historical context* in which they're used. What enabled the creation of symbols was not just the large human brain, Greenfeld says, but the larynx, what we call the voice box, a small organ in the top of the neck that lets us manipulate sound with far more nuance than other animals. At some unknowable point in our evolutionary past, early *Homo sapiens* realized they could create sounds that had no intrinsic meaning, aside from the meaning they chose to give it at that specific point in time. They created words, and words generate more words, until a whole system of symbols emerges: a language.

Unlike our ability to read and react to signs, language isn't encoded into our DNA. We don't pass it down genetically—but we do pass it down. Since the invention of language, humans have been born into an elaborate *symbolic reality*. Almost all of this reality was created by those who came before, but it never ceases to evolve, and every new person can change it. This symbolic reality is what we mean when we use the word "culture." When a child enters the culture by acquiring language, her mind is born.

It's a feedback loop: the mind creates culture, and culture creates each new mind. The brain makes both possible, but culture and mind are not material like the brain. They create material by-products, like books and rockets and iPhones, but there is "no material aspect to [their] actual happening."

As Greenfeld explains, and this is the crucial point, *the mind is a process, a function of time.*

Just like language and culture. We can't know what a word means unless you specify *when* it's being used. The meanings of words change, sometimes dramatically, over time. Similarly, to understand the value of anything in culture, we have to put it in temporal context. It's the same with us. We remember into the past, hope into the future. We see ourselves through a temporal lens. "I am not who I was *back then*," we say. "I'm different *now*."

Think about it: there is no physicality to our thoughts. They don't take up space (even if we sometimes use that metaphor to describe them). Thoughts happen in sequence, in time.

Greenfeld's theory of mind casts our internet addictions in a different light. When we give away time, it implies, we give away ourselves. When we spend hours scrolling Facebook, we are literally swapping our own thoughts for the feed's. In fact, through the lens of this theory, much of the social internet starts to *resemble* a human mind, for what is a mind if not a timeline? In the timelines of Facebook, TikTok, Snapchat, I see approximations of mental life: columns of posts, ordered by when they were published, meant to be read, seen, or watched in sequence.

In Twitter, I see the closest approximation of all: a simple timeline of posts in the dominant symbolic system of language, each as brief as a thought. Tweets look like thoughts, don't they? They are short, fragmentary, often poorly considered, sometimes funny, sometimes nonsensical, usually suffused with emotion. They come and go quickly as whims, flitting down the timeline, always yielding to the next, and the next. You can have your own thoughts while reading Twitter, but why bother?

The other thing Greenfeld's theory implies is that the border between culture and individual minds is porous. We're already thinking with a language we didn't invent, with knowledge we didn't generate, with conventional wisdom established long before we were born. How many of our ideas are original? How many are influenced by our parents, by what we've read, by what our parents read? Culture is always in the mind, and the internet is just an expression of culture. An internet séance like the *Cats* one I recorded above is an extension of ordinary thinking.

It's *how much* of an extension that troubles me. Culture guides us, but there is such a thing as agency. Individuals get their symbols from culture, but we can choose how to put them together. That's the work of thinking, the source of new ideas on which an evolving culture depends. Every mind can add to the symbolic commonwealth.

When I'm consuming the internet, it feels like the agency dial has been turned to zero. Culture isn't just in my mind; it's *steering* my thinking. I'm no longer the one putting the symbols together. Twitter's algorithm is doing it for me, or Facebook's, or Google's. And as I spend more time online, I'm getting better at ascertaining the internet's opinions, instead of developing my own. That's what I was doing with the *Cats* trailer, scouring the web like an investigative reporter trying to piece together the opinions of other people. So I could—what? Adopt those opinions? Parrot those opinions when someone eventually asked me what I thought about the trailer? Or was I doing it because, well, that's just what we do on social media?

After I watch a YouTube video or see an Instagram post, I instinctively scroll to the comments to see what others think. The number of likes and dislikes offers me a ready-made judgment. When you're moving hurriedly from post to post, those judgments are handy—until you reach the end of the day and realize they comprise most of your point of view. You lie in bed and wonder: What do *I* think?

But then you doze off.

Don't get me wrong: you can learn a lot on the internet. You can learn more than at any previous time in history. But ingesting information is only half of learning. The other half, the more important half, is *responding* to that information, thinking critically about it, about what it implies. Does it fit with your worldview? If not, why not? This is the part of learning that turns knowledge into wisdom, into action. This is the part of learning through which you create yourself, and it demands mental free time, time when you're not consuming media of any kind, when you're doing nothing at all. By greedily claiming every appointment on your mind's timeline, the internet erases these vital hours from your life.

I learned this lesson making The Nerdwriter. Over the last decade, I've produced about 250 episodes of my YouTube series. Writing the show can be difficult, editing is time-consuming—but my biggest obstacle has always been coming up with original ideas. For years, my instinct was to scour the internet for something noteworthy and exclusive, something that struck a chord with me. I'd read for hours and hours, but then I'd come to the end of the day and have nothing to show for it, aside from irritated eyes and a mild headache. A week might pass like this. I would get so frustrated that I'd give up, go for lunch, take a walk, do the laundry I'd been putting off. Then, BAM! While I was folding a piece of underwear, listening to some Jessie Ware, an idea would appear! It took me way too long to realize what you can no doubt already see: I needed to include free time, nothing time, in this period of ideation. Research is important, but constantly being an input is not conducive to invention. I needed to let my mind do its thing.

And the mind will, if you let it. Weird things. Impressive things. Scary things. When was the last time you sat facing a window for forty-five minutes? It's tougher than it sounds. Whenever I try it, I sit there for what feels like two hours, only to glance at the clock to see six minutes have passed. "Nothing time" runs at a snail's pace—at least one-tenth the rate of Twitter time and one-thirtieth the rate of TikTok time. And your mind doesn't always wander where you want it to. Often it wanders right into your anxieties, that mirror maze in the basement of your personality. Once I began to carve out time for doing nothing, I found myself in that maze a lot. It's an uncomfortable place to be. So many years with instant access to distraction crippled the natural defenses I had to deal with that stuff, to process it. You have to be prepared to withstand a good amount of self-punishment if you want to reclaim time for yourself.

But the rewards are worth it—and not just for those who work in the creative arts. All work benefits from fresh thinking. Personal growth depends on new ideas. The internet of today, designed to make you a permanent input, does more than just steal time from you; it erodes your agency and substitutes internet-awareness for self-awareness. Those are the three things—time, agency, and self-awareness—that we use to construct our identities. Without them, sense of self weakens, identity destabilizes, and the result is what we see in the research and feel in ourselves: stress, anxiety, or worse.

Despite awareness of the problem, despite the constant media coverage, despite all the tortured PR from tech companies, I don't expect any real change to the time-eating incentive structure of the internet in the near term. Maybe I'm just a pessimist. Maybe the backlash to Big Tech's invasive practices will translate into action sooner than later. You can already hear the rumbling of a political coalition that cuts across party lines on this issue. And there are some impressive people out there sitting silently in front of their windows, imagining new ways to design the internet business model, to break social media's addiction to our addiction.

But the gap between awareness and change is vast. A little less than a month ago, when I began writing this essay, I was earnestly committed to cutting down my tech use. I trapped my iPhone in the closet and checked for messages only once or twice per day, never bringing it into the bedroom. I deleted all the social media apps. I sat dutifully in my chair each morning and watched cars go by, letting my insecurities batter me. It wasn't fun, but it let up after a while. I had some good ideas, did some productive work. My mind felt quiet. It felt like mine.

A month later and that's all out the window. My iPhone is right here, next to my laptop. I check it once a minute, give or take. It sleeps beside me, on my nightstand, and I open it immediately upon waking. All those apps have been re-downloaded. My screen time graph looks like a giant U, with new peaks threatening to exceed the old ones. Sunday at nine a.m. is once again the Hour of Shame. Work continues because it has to, but I'm far less productive. Anyone who's tried to confront their internet addiction will be familiar with this kind of backsliding. I can't even recall what broke my good habits or when it happened. It snuck up on me. Now I have to regroup. I have to put those safeguards back in place to retake control of my mind.

But I don't have to do that yet, do I?

No, not yet.

THE COMFORTS OF CYBERPUNK

About thirty-five minutes into *Blade Runner*, there's a short scene in which Rick Deckard, a recently unretired cop who hunts and kills rogue androids, takes a glass of whiskey onto the terrace of his apartment, ninety-seven floors above the ground. The camera shows the terrace in profile, and behind it, a monstrous, kaleidoscopic city of the future: flying cars, neon ads, a billion glittering lights. Deckard shivers under the blanket on his shoulders, drinks, Vangelis's score pulses to life. The impression is one of deep alienation and loneliness, of a little man in his little box in a city full of an infinite number of the same.

To me, it feels comforting.

That's a peculiar response to *Blade Runner*, I know—maybe even a little concerning. Comfort doesn't go with dystopia. A "comfortable dystopia" is an oxymoron, a dystopia that's not doing its job right. What about this bleak vision of a cyberpunk Los Angeles could possibly be *desirable* to me?

And not only me. As a subgenre and an aesthetic,

cyberpunk has proven to be enduringly desirable. *Blade Runner* premiered in 1982, forty years ago. The future it depicts is now in our past. Like the original cyberpunk novels, which debuted around the same time, *Blade Runner* is unmistakably eighties in spirit, reacting to the conditions of that era, extrapolating its future from the tech and politics of the time. Four decades removed, we're still making cyberpunk art in the same spirit—and I don't just mean the 2017 *Blade Runner* sequel, *Blade Runner 2049*. Think of Duncan Jones's 2018 film, *Mute*, or Lisa Joy's *Reminiscence* from 2021, or the recent Netflix series *Altered Carbon*, based on the 2002 cyberpunk novel by Richard K. Morgan. These are not small projects. *Altered Carbon* reportedly cost $7 million per episode, while *Blade Runner 2049* was somewhere in the ballpark of $185 million. If studios are willing to hand over that much cash for cyberpunk entertainment, they must believe there's broad demand for it.

And if movies, television, and books aren't immersive enough for you, no worries: in late 2020, CD Projekt Red released *Cyberpunk 2077*, a vast open-world video game, where you can explore the seedy yet vibrant Night City as V, a technologically enhanced mercenary who is fully customizable (down to the genitals). Follow the game's branching narrative or cruise Night City at your leisure. If you ever wanted to get lost in a "real" cyberpunk universe, this game is your ticket. Judging by the tidal wave of preorders, it looks like I'm far from the only one who finds this stuff alluring.*

---

* A few months after I wrote this essay, *Cyberpunk 2077* had one of the most disastrous game releases in recent memory, due to a variety of glitches and bugs. It was a bummer. Enthusiasm for the game declined rapidly. Even so, the immense excitement *ahead* of its release speaks to cyberpunk's enduring appeal.

So—what is "this stuff," exactly?

I've called cyberpunk a subgenre and an aesthetic. I think the latter is easier to identify than the former is to define. That's because cyberpunk has seeded elements of its style into the cultural imagination. I can't walk down a rainy city street at night without feeling like I'm Rick Deckard. Steaming food stalls in crowded open-air markets, dance concerts in old industrial warehouses, the way neon flickers off wet asphalt—cyberpunk has totally colonized my experience of neon. Scraps of this visual language can be found all across pop culture, from *The Matrix* and *Ghost in the Shell* to works less explicitly influenced by the genre, like the recent James Bond movie *Skyfall* or Coldplay's 2021 music video for "Higher Power." Need a gritty urban space of the future? Cyberpunk is your palette. The aesthetic is familiar to the point of cliché. In other words, we know it when we see it.

What cyberpunk actually is, as a science fiction subgenre and art movement, is more complicated. It has roots in the New Wave science fiction of the sixties and seventies, in which writers like J. G. Ballard and Michael Moorcock brought experimental ambitions to an often formulaic genre. The New Wave reacted against science fiction's Golden Age, in which heroes wielding shiny gadgets traveled on shiny ships with shiny robots to shiny cities in outer space. Those swashbuckling voyagers lacked psychological depth, they felt; those techno-utopias lacked political realism.

In 1962, Ballard argued for discarding the space story entirely: "The biggest developments of the immediate future," he wrote, "will take place, not on the Moon or Mars, but on

Earth, and it is inner space, not outer, that needs to be explored." Ballard's "inner space" was a surreal and scary place, enlarged by the global media network that was beginning to dominate human experience. As Rob Latham points out, New Wave authors engaged with a number of themes—the impacts of new information technologies and the ways a capitalist system might control them, the possibility of uploading consciousness to virtual spaces, the proliferation of synthetic realities and simulated experiences—that their cyberpunk successors would take up and synthesize in a new literary movement for a new decade.

With a new approach, too.

Cyberpunk authors prized the physical. They embedded their ideas in worlds of immense, dusty detail, settings so tactile you can feel the vibrations of off-world ships coming to port in Chiba City, hear the whine of an antique mechanical arm "cased in grubby pink plastic." Technology is everywhere in these stories, but it's invasive, malfunctioning, greasy. And that materiality reflects the decade when this fiction emerged.

"Eighties tech sticks to the skin," wrote Bruce Sterling in his preface to the 1986 cyberpunk anthology *Mirrorshades*. "The personal computer, the Sony Walkman, the portable telephone, the soft contact lens." Sterling describes the "visceral" impression this tech had on his circle of writers and how that prompted the "garage-band aesthetic" of their prose—a style less cultivated, less openly literary, than that of their New Wave predecessors, but purposefully so. It had a raw quality, like the punk music from which the movement takes half its name.

Cyberpunks married a "hard sf" approach to technology (cyber) with a subcultural perspective (punk). Or as Sterling puts it: "An unholy alliance of the technical world and the world of organized dissent—the underground world of pop culture, visionary fluidity and street-level anarchy."

Or, more simply: high tech, low life.

Faceless multinational corporations rule these futures, but the stories take place on the streets in endless urban sprawl, where small-time crooks and marginalized loners repurpose the overflow of tech to make their scores, to sow chaos in virtual systems, or just to get high. Bodies fuse with machines, brains mesh with ports that link them to the other essential backdrop of this subgenre: *cyberspace*.

Cyberspace is a familiar concept now—nearly synonymous with "internet"—but it wasn't when William Gibson coined the term in 1982, in a short story called "Burning Chrome." Two years later, he defined "cyberspace" in his debut novel, *Neuromancer*:

A consensual hallucination experienced daily by billions of legitimate operators, in every nation . . . a graphic representation of data abstracted from the banks of every computer in the human system. Unthinkable complexity. Lines of light ranged in the nonspace of the mind, clusters and constellations of data. Like city lights, receding.

In *Neuromancer*, hackers, known as "console cowboys" jack into cyberspace and infiltrate the private networks of governments or multinationals, lifting data for cash. The digital space Gibson devised doesn't quite resemble the web of today, but is there a better two-word description for the modern internet than "consensual hallucination"?

Gibson is far from the only important cyberpunk writer (others from that first wave include Sterling, Rudy Rucker, and Pat Cadigan), but *Neuromancer* and the Sprawl stories that accompany it are quintessential texts. Most of the things we associate with the subgenre—hackers, cyberspace, urban sprawl, body modification, artificial intelligence, neon and neo-noir, alienation and societal decay—can be found in them. In the same way that romantic love can't be defined any more succinctly than *Romeo and Juliet*, *Neuromancer* itself is probably the simplest way to define cyberpunk. If someone wants to know what it is, just hand them the book.

Or take them to see *Blade Runner*.

If *Neuromancer* is the quintessential cyberpunk novel, *Blade Runner* is the quintessential cyberpunk film. I first saw it in college. Since then I've seen it more times than I can count, in full or in part, to the point where it no longer feels like watching, but *tapping into* a familiar texture and rhythm. Extraordinary films transport you into their worlds, but with Ridley Scott's *Blade Runner* it was the opposite: the world of the film transported into me.

Blade Runner came out two years before *Neuromancer*, but one year after "Johnny Mnemonic," the first of Gibson's Sprawl stories. The two universes don't cover exactly the same ground, but the overlap is uncanny. They both feature anarchic, decadent settings of the future, spilling over with people, tech, and detritus from various eras. The skylines in both are overshadowed by megastructures controlled by megacorporations. They both draw from film noir (*Blade Runner* is a detective story and *Neuromancer* is a heist) and channel its cynical mode. Both star classic noir antiheroes: hardboiled and burnt-out underlings past their prime. Both examine the nature of humanity through artificial intelligences. Both incorporate Asian influences, the roaring high-tech Tokyo of the eighties, the dense settlements of Kowloon Walled City in Hong Kong. They're both rain-soaked, gripped by unceasing violence, haunted by an overwhelming ennui, awash in neon.

Gibson walked out of *Blade Runner* after ten minutes: "I reeled out of the theater in complete despair over its visual brilliance and its similarity to the 'look' of *Neuromancer*, my largely unwritten first novel. Not only had I been beaten to the semiotic punch, but this damned movie looked better than the images in my head!" After all the work it takes to come up with something original, it must be maddening to find that another artist has arrived at the same place independently.

Years later, when Gibson and Scott finally had lunch and compared influences, both acknowledged the debt they owed to *Métal Hurlant*, a French comics magazine helmed by artist Jean Giraud, better known as Mœbius. And if you look at "The Long Tomorrow" from 1976, a story drawn by Mœbius and written by Dan O'Bannon, you can see the first flowering of what would soon become the cluttered cyberpunk aesthetic.

Precursors don't stop there, of course. *Blade Runner* is based on Philip K. Dick's 1968 novel *Do Androids*

Dream of Electric Sheep?, considered by many a "proto-cyberpunk" work—a designation that also includes William Burroughs's *Naked Lunch* and Alfred Bester's *The Stars My Destination*, as well as movies like Fritz Lang's *Metropolis* and John Carpenter's *Escape from New York*. Gibson has cited the hardboiled detective fiction of Dashiell Hammett, the postmodern satires of Thomas Pynchon, and the disaffected lyrics of Lou Reed as touchstones for *Neuromancer*. Cyberpunk is built from many parts. It's as much a collage as the cities and people it depicts.

In fact, collage is probably its keynote. You can see the urban sites of cyberpunk fiction—the Sprawl, Neo Tokyo, Los Angeles 2019—as physical manifestations of the "cut-up technique" that William Burroughs pioneered in the fifties and sixties. Burroughs *literally* cut up passages of prose and pasted them back together at random, creating a collage of strange and often shocking juxtapositions. Look at how he assembles his images in *Naked Lunch*, the colors and textures, the specificity:

> We pour it in a Pernod and start for New Orleans past iridescent lakes and orange gas flares, and swamps and garbage heaps, alligators crawling around in broken bottles and tin cans, neon arabesques of motels, marooned pimps scream obscenities at passing cars from islands of rubbish.

Compare that to Gibson's description of the Sprawl in *Count Zero*:

Silent figures sat beside spread blankets as they
passed; the blankets arrayed with surreal assort-
ments of merchandise: damp-swollen cardboard
covers of black plastic audio disks beside battered
prosthetic limbs trailing crude nerve jacks, a dusty
glass fishbowl filled with oblong steel dog tags,
rubber-banded stacks of faded postcards, cheap
Indo trodes still sealed in wholesaler's plastic . . .

Cyberpunk cities are vast collages where strange and
often shocking juxtapositions await on every corner. The
language Gibson uses to describe his fictional metropolis
"cuts up" mundane debris with techno-speak. The future
folded into the past, and vice versa. "Cities are like compost
heaps," he told *The Paris Review* in 2011. "Just layers and
layers of stuff. In cities, the past and the present and the
future can all be totally adjacent."

Among other things, Burroughs's disjointed prose
aimed to snap people out of conformity. He used the jarring
contrasts of collage to short-circuit language's tendency to
reproduce oppressive narratives—in his case, the conservative values of postwar America. By the eighties those values
had exploded, but Gibson found this technique useful for
different reasons. For him, the hallucinatory mishmash of
stuff captured something true about experience in the new
information age: the vertigo of accelerating change, the
dizzying spectacle of globalized media, the feeling of being
drowned in consumer goods with barely a shelf life before
obsolescence. Disjointed imagery had power because life
was disjointed—and because we were.

Maybe that's why these stories comfort me. Cyberpunk turns those messy feelings into a place, where it's no longer necessary to resist the splintering pressures of society because the fight's over and we lost. All that's left is to submit to the carnival of sensations. In a cyberpunk future, I can let go. I can melt into the prismatic flux of civilization. There's a relief in that, even a feeling of oneness.

Think of the monologue Roy Batty delivers at the end of *Blade Runner*. Moments before dying, the replicant Batty laments the loss of his unique experiences in the amnesia of time:

> I've seen things you people wouldn't believe. Attack ships on fire off the shoulder of Orion. I watched C-beams glitter in the dark near the Tannhäuser Gate. All those moments will be lost in time, like tears in rain.

It's one of the most evocative speeches in film history, made more so by the visual of a rain-soaked Batty and the tears we can't see, underscored by Vangelis's music. It captures existential anxieties we all share. I have a kindred feeling when I look into the night sky. Nothing makes me feel smaller than imagining the space between galaxies, or the time it takes for a star's light to reach my eye. But while there is angst in this line of thinking, there is also a blissful feeling of surrender. Part of me is calmed by my insignificance, by the teardrop of my life being lost in the downpour of time.

I feel the same way in big cities, where I can fade into

the crowd, into the lights and noise, into "sanctioned delirium," as the poet Charles Baudelaire put it. I came across Baudelaire searching for others who share this feeling of surrender, this attraction to cities. He describes something similar in his concept of the *flâneur*.

From the French word for "stroller," a flâneur is someone at home in the swarm of city streets. "It is an immense joy to set up house in the heart of the multitude," Baudelaire writes, "amid the ebb and flow of movement, in the midst of the fugitive and the infinite." Baudelaire was the flâneur par excellence of nineteenth-century Paris, as he wandered through arcades, department stores, across wide boulevards lit by gas lamps, observing, vanishing. Baudelaire's flâneur is a figure of thoughtful observation, but one who is also marked by an encroaching loss of self, "an 'I' with an insatiable appetite for the 'non-I.'"

The flâneur is also a product of "modernity," a term Baudelaire coined to describe "the transient, the fleeting, the contingent" experience of life in the nineteenth century, a transitional period during which the modern metropolis emerged—as well as the unique psychological afflictions it gave rise to.

The chaos of urban centers "stimulates the nerves to their utmost reactivity," wrote sociologist Georg Simmel in an influential essay from 1903, "until they can finally produce no reaction at all." As anyone who's lived in a city will know, it's easy to feel overstimulated, and too much of that feeling can render you numb and disconnected from the people around you, even from yourself. "The deep problems of modern life," Simmel wrote, "flow from the attempt of the individual to maintain the independence and individuality of his existence against the sovereign powers of the society." If the city dweller fails to do so, they're at risk of "being leveled, swallowed up in the social-technological mechanism" of the metropolis.

Simmel and those who came after rightly deemed this potential loss of self a danger—maybe *the* danger of greater urbanism. A century later, these alienating forces have only grown more severe. Cities got bigger and more complex. Relationships became more impersonal, more mediated by money and technology, more transactional. All along the way there were theorists analyzing these trends, and artists offering poignant portraits of urban alienation: books like J. D. Salinger's *The Catcher in the Rye*, movies like Martin Scorsese's *Taxi Driver*, songs like the Kinks' "Waterloo Sunset," paintings like Edward Hopper's *Nighthawks*. Many of these works present alienation as a psychological rot, and it can certainly be that. The city's special brand of loneliness is often crippling. It can exacerbate antisocial tendencies in a vicious loop, resulting in anxiety, depression, and violence, like Travis Bickle's bloody rampage in the final minutes of *Taxi Driver*. There's no question that the metropolis has curdled its share of souls.

But there's a flip side to this fact. Isolation, rootlessness, anonymity: the negative connotations of these are obvious, but they are not *necessarily* bad. Similarly, the close bonds you find in small communities, though they may provide stability, are not necessarily good. The ties in communities like that can be tight to the point of suffocating, as I'm sure many of you know. The roots people have there can be restrictive to the point of paralysis. In this case, rootlessness might be longed for. Anonymity might feel like liberation, isolation like relief. For the same reasons that a city can be alienating, it can also be a site of freedom. For Baudelaire's flâneur, the loss of self is not agony, but ecstasy. He becomes a "kaleidoscope gifted with consciousness" in "an immense reservoir of electrical energy." Even Simmel acknowledges that the metropolis "assures the individual of a type and degree of personal freedom to which there is no analogy in other circumstances."

This is another reason cyberpunk comforts me. The cities of cyberpunk are fantasy zones where the responsibilities of everyday life, the expectations of relationships and community, are absent. There are no true friends there, just brief acquaintances who pass in and out of your life according to their use. Case, the protagonist of *Neuromancer*, has no family to speak of, neither does any of his associates. Rick Deckard is much the same: friendless and family-less—until he meets Rachael, that is. Like a million other lost souls in a million other Hollywood movies, their salvation from this alienated universe is each other. Case has no such luck. His romances are purely sexual, affairs of self-interest, fading as they begin.

You may think, reading this, that I'd like to abandon all my relationships and disappear into the Sprawl. Let me reassure my wife, family, and friends before I start getting concerned calls: that is *not* the case. Deep relationships are the only lasting source of happiness, in my opinion, and, along with some meaningful work and pastries, all

I really need. What's more, if I actually were to be transported into *Blade Runner*'s world, I'd probably beg to return to my life within a few days, if not hours. Fantasies of escape are laughably superficial. Under the gentlest pressure, they collapse. Chase after them, and they retreat. If somehow you attain the fantasy, it dissipates or changes aspect. You desired *desiring* them, you discover, not the thing itself.

Life is not a zero-sum game between the freedoms of isolation and the stability of relationships, but there is some sacrifice of one for the other. I'm married, involved with my friends, close with my parents. I wouldn't change that, but it does mean I forgo some freedoms. I can't vanish for a week and not tell anyone. I can barely go that long without calling my mom! In certain ways, we're all limited by the people in our networks—by their image of us, their expectations, their needs. In the last decade, I've learned just how much the benefits of good relationships outweigh their drawbacks, yet it doesn't surprise me that I sometimes fantasize about life without these limitations, that I want it both ways. For me, the city has always been the locus of this fantasy, the cyberpunk city its purest distillation.

As dystopias go, cyberpunk is unique. The Los Angeles of *Blade Runner* may be a grim place in theory—filthy, harsh, sharply stratified—but Ridley Scott's camera suffuses it with lyricism. Even scenes of violence, like the one in which Deckard shoots down the replicant Zhora in the street, are intensely poetic:

Zhora crashes through shopwindows as Deckard's bullet shatters her shoulder. She cries out, then falls in slow motion, shards of glass raining over her. Vangelis's synthesizers echo. With failing strength, Zhora manages to rise, only to be pierced by a second bullet, launching her through a retail display of gently falling snow. Momentum carries her into the street, where she collapses onto a bed of shattered mirrors that reflect the multicolored neon of an indifferent city.

It's an unforgettable sequence of images in a film full of them. Scott and his collaborators render their dystopia as dreamworld. The movie has a hypnotic pace, an elegiac tone. Its narrative is subordinate to the mise-en-scène—which is not to say the story is unimportant, only that the movie's aesthetic experience is emotional in itself. *Blade Runner* is a Romantic work of art, in other words, or "Dark Romantic," in the tradition of Edgar Allan Poe and noir. As poet April Bernard said, "Noir is romanticism embittered. The life of feeling that has been betrayed leads to the attitude and genre of noir. No one who loves noir is a cynic. Cynics never believed in anything in the first place. People who love noir are disillusioned romantics." *Blade Runner* makes beautiful the tragedy of its future, and that beauty invites the viewer. It creates an ideal container for escapist fantasies about the metropolis.

Using different tools, like the collage technique I described above, literary cyberpunk achieves its own kind of lyricism. Like *Blade Runner*'s L.A., its settings are grimy yet dazzling, brutal yet attractive. Most of all, they're *cool*. Where does cool come from if not "the underground world of pop culture," which was baked into cyberpunk's DNA from the start? The novels explore these subcultures more extensively than cyberpunk films do. Their characters are stranger and more diverse, more representative of the "visionary fluidity" Sterling describes. In these scrambled futures, traditional categories of identification get scrambled, too—so if you're someone who feels hemmed in by labels, not quite captured by the in-groups of this reality, cyberpunk might offer an escape, a place where you can construct an identity like a cyberspace hacker retrofits her body with machine parts.

This is what Donna Haraway hopes in her seminal essay "A Cyborg Manifesto," from 1985. For Haraway, the cyborg represents a possible escape from binaries of gender and sexuality, toward more dynamic forms of identity creation, toward "*pleasure* in the confusion of boundaries." How well cyberpunk made good on that potential is up for debate, but the idea has been a draw for many of its readers and viewers. It still is. Look, for example, at the extreme customizability in *Cyberpunk 2077*'s character creator. When constructing your avatar, you can mix and match traits from across the gender spectrum, with no requirement to choose a sex at the outset. Earlier in development, the game *did* force that choice, but the designers removed it after feedback from those who wanted to play as characters who reflected their own fluid and visionary selves.

The asphalt of cyberpunk is fertile for escapes—from the fragmenting pressures of modern culture, from the stifling expectations of relationships, from reductive categories of identification. While it's an environment ravaged by exploitation and crime and inequality, it's also a massive sandbox of possibility and freedom and fun. Decades ago, cyberpunk may have mounted an effective critique against cultural and political trends, but its writers and filmmakers made their dystopias too enchanting. As we get further from the 1980s, the critique loses its bite and the enchantment becomes fantasy and, finally, nostalgia. This is why it endures. Cyberpunk is a false future, a future of the past. In its playground, we are free to be reckless and selfish and shortsighted and lost. We are free not to care, not to fight, not to matter.

There may be cyberspace in cyberpunk, but there's no social media. There may be surveillance, but there's resistance to it. Who could have guessed in the 1980s that we would choose to surveil ourselves, that we would happily give up every crumb of personal information for packages delivered a few days sooner and tailored search results? Cyberpunk offers a nostalgic escape from what is dystopic in our present, not by appealing to some idealized past, but by imagining an alternate timeline in which those things never came to pass.

Set in 2019, *Blade Runner* is no longer the future. It's now, another now. I wouldn't choose it over ours, but that only amplifies its appeal.

WHEN EXPERTS DISAGREE

The world is crowded with people who are *certain*. You see them on the news, at the pulpit; you hear them at dinner parties and neighborhood cafés. These people *know*, or act like they do. They know the answers to the most difficult questions, they know the actions that need to be taken. They know why the wrong choices are wrong and the right choices are right, and in private maybe they doubt but in public they're *sure*, sure this candidate should be elected and this advice should be heeded, and if only you did *this*, then *that* would happen, without question. At times, I am one of these people. I'm guilty of telling friends what they should do, even when I don't have all the info, even when I have all the info but the situation is too complex for any one solution to be as right as I'm making it seem.

It's usually better to talk less and listen more, and if I don't always take that advice in personal matters, in political ones I have, to the point of radio silence—especially in the last few years. The biggest reason for that is my job. As my audience has grown at The Nerdwriter, I've felt more and more responsible for being right, and more and more fearful of being wrong. With complicated issues, the risk often seems too great, so I opt for making videos about subjects that invite varied interpretation, like works of art. My analysis of a painting or film is not Right with a capital R; it's just one reading among many. And if my take on *Blade Runner* or Goya's *Saturn Devouring His Son* helps you appreciate the work in a new way, if it helps you see those masterpieces from a different angle, I'm satisfied. On issues that require true expertise, that do have a Right answer, I've become much more cautious.

This responsibility, that fear, forced me to reevaluate my beliefs. As a result, some of my opinions were reinforced, while others were challenged and had to be changed. It always feels good to learn that you're right, and it's never easy to admit you're wrong, but in both cases, at least you arrive at an answer. What's more upsetting than either of these is a dead end, and it's these dead ends I want to explore in this essay. They can be summed up in a question that's haunted me for a long time:

When experts disagree, how do I decide?

When those who have spent their entire working lives trying to understand an issue cannot find consensus, how does the layperson determine what is right?

Debates rage in every discipline, from philosophy to physics to art to planktology. In subjective fields, experts can be helpful, but they're not necessary to establish what's good and bad. As I suggested before, there are no Right answers in art criticism, just opinions—some more insightful than others, but even the most insightful aren't binding. We can all decide for ourselves what has artistic value.

In highly specialized fields, on the other hand, like astrophysics, expertise is a precondition for comment. I could give my view on why there are discrepancies in the Hubble constant, but that view is unlikely to have any impact on working astrophysicists. Fortunately for science, I'm not responsible for making judgments on esoteric debates like this, nor is any layperson.

It's not art or astrophysics that keeps me up at night; it's politics. All the esoteric debates that fall under its umbrella *actually are* my responsibility. Representative democracies ask citizens to weigh in on extremely complex issues by choosing politicians who will enact policies that might affect thousands, millions, even hundreds of millions of people. To vote is to come down on one side of a debate. We can outsource some of the strategy to our representatives, but *we* are the final authority. On huge questions of economics, health, war, and justice, the buck stops with me, with you. If this is the system we want, that's the responsibility we have.

No pressure.

Obviously it's impossible for any one person to become an expert on every subject about which they're asked to vote. Even if I filtered issues through the narrowest self-interest, I would still have plenty of difficulty making choices. Do I favor or oppose the Authorization for Use of Military Force, for example, which allows the president to undertake war against al-Qaeda and its affiliates without congressional approval? Is that authorization good or bad for me? The powers it grants could enable the president to act with the speed necessary to stop a terror attack that could hurt me or someone I love. On the flip side, those powers could be used to justify engagement in conflicts I oppose, putting a servicemember friend in harm's way, or depleting so much of the federal budget that programs I need go underfunded. At first glance, after *many* glances, I find it unclear which position benefits me most. It's even less clear which position benefits everyone most. All I really know is that I'm unqualified to choose.

So I research. I learn. I turn to the experts.

In the modern era, knowledge has become so vast and specialized that a lifetime of study won't scratch the surface. Informed citizens have no choice but to depend on the expertise of others, and the essential skill in today's world is not so much learning as *filtering*, sifting through those who claim to be knowledgeable about a subject, then choosing whom to believe.

We expend our critical thinking on reputation as much as information: Where is this data coming from? What are the credentials of this person or group? Do they have an agenda? What have colleagues said about them? Do people you trust *trust* this person, this organization, this theory, this finding? Do a majority of the people in the field believe this to be true? An overwhelming majority? Why does the minority disagree? Broad knowledge in a specialized world can be achieved only by means of trust.

After all, what do I really know about climate change? If I'm honest with myself, I have to admit that my support for policies to fight climate change rests on the fact that basically all scientists believe it to be real, dangerous, driven by human activity, and capable of being mitigated. I learned that from science educators, who are essential links between experts and laypeople, but that's a couple degrees of separation from figures and experiments. I couldn't tell you anything about those experiments, or how they yield the data that make all those troubling graphs. I probably shouldn't source my climate knowledge solely from John Oliver, who told me on *Last Week Tonight* that "a survey of thousands of scientific papers that took a position on climate change found that 97 percent endorsed the position that humans are causing global warming," but how far down does my responsibility go?

A few layers more at least.

The survey Oliver mentioned, "Quantifying the Consensus on Anthropogenic Global Warming in the Scientific Literature," comes from *Environmental Research Letters*, a quarterly, peer-reviewed, open-access scientific journal covering all aspects of environmental science. It's one of many academic journals published by the Institute of Physics, a 145-year-old "scientific charity that works to advance physics education, research and application." Trying to get a sense of the bona fides of these groups, I came across the concept of impact factors, a metric used to calculate the credibility and significance of academic journals. *Environmental Research Letters* has an impact factor of 6.192, according to the *2019 Journal Citations Reports*, a widely cited publication by Clarivate Analytics, putting it in the top tier of environmental science journals.

Okay, the source is legit. What does the study say?

The survey analyzed 11,944 climate abstracts from peer-reviewed papers that matched search results of "global warming" or "global climate change," and it covered a twenty-one-year period, from 1991 to 2012. Independent researchers were randomly assigned the abstracts and asked to rate them categorically (the aspect of climate science involved) and by degree of endorsement (of the idea that climate change is real and caused by humans). Each abstract was rated independently by two researchers. If there was a disagreement, they compared opinions and justified their choices. If they still disagreed, a third party was brought in to make the final call.

The authors consolidated the results into three categories: **endorsement, no position**, and **rejection**. Of the 11,944 abstracts,

- 32.6 percent **endorsed** the idea of man-made global warming
- 66.4 percent offered **no position**
- 0.7 percent **rejected** the idea and 0.3 percent **expressed uncertainty**

So where does the 97 percent come from? The authors don't say that 97 percent of *all* abstracts endorse the position that humans are causing global warming, *but 97 percent of those expressing an opinion.* To get that figure, they put aside the 66.4 percent of papers that offered no position, calculating that 97.1 percent of the remaining papers maintain climate change is real and caused by us.

Does this mean the 66.4 percent of abstracts expressing no opinion are still on the fence? The authors anticipated this question and reached out to these scientists personally. The majority of those who responded believed their paper did in fact endorse man-made climate change. Only 1.8 percent of self-raters said their work rejected the idea, mirroring the initial findings. Additionally, the authors explain that a large percentage of no-position papers is consistent with consensus situations, where the fundamental science is "no longer controversial among the publishing science community and the remaining debate in the field has moved to other topics."

This survey is the most-read entry in the history of *Environmental Research Letters*, downloaded over a million times. After two more days of researching, I couldn't find any paper from an equally reputable journal that refuted its core findings. The closest thing to a challenge I discovered was a reply by Richard Tol, also published in *Environmental Research Letters*, which argued that faults in the survey's methodology overestimated the consensus—but did not dispute the idea of man-made climate change. If you accounted for these mistakes, Tol suggests, the consensus value would be closer to 91 percent. The original authors rebutted this rebuttal, defending their methods. In another reply, geologist James Powell also debated the methodology, but found the opposite result: according to his reading of the abstracts, 99.9 percent of climate scientists agree with man-made global warming, "verging on unanimity." The original authors rebutted this rebuttal, too.

When a consensus is this overwhelming, do you have a responsibility to seek out the vanishingly small number of dissenting opinions? It's important to be sensitive to your own biases—and to recognize that those biases can manifest in subtle ways; in how you phrase a Google search, for example—but I believe there's a point at which additional research is unnecessary. We're taught to weigh all sides of a debate, but when does a debate stop being a debate? Could any layperson really say that data from the survey's 118 contrarian climate papers outweigh the consensus in 3,896 others?

Later in that *Last Week Tonight* segment, Oliver describes the irresponsible ways man-made climate change is presented as debatable. When the "debate" is covered on television, he says, "it's always one person for, one person against. . . . When you look at the screen, it's fifty-fifty, which is inherently misleading. If there has to be a debate about the reality of climate change—*and there doesn't*—then there is only one mathematically fair way to do it." He then stages a "statistically representative climate change debate," pitting three climate change deniers against Bill Nye and ninety-six other scientists.

I'm convinced. A combination of research and common sense tells me that global warming *is* real and *is* caused by human activity. Whether it's dangerous, exactly how dangerous, and how much we can mitigate the effects at this point are separate questions. Following the standards I used above, I found that the harms of climate change are significant and will worsen over time. I'm also convinced there are steps we could take to alleviate those harms (though not completely) and that inaction will be very damaging. I'm not detailing my research on these questions in the same way I detailed the survey above, but you can check my sources in the works cited section.

Or you could just trust me.

You could trust my trust, that is. I still know very little about the fieldwork of climatologists, the data science involved, or the predictive models they use. My knowledge of climate history is basic, as is my knowledge of weather patterns, polar ice caps, academic publishing, peer review, and so much more. I also don't know what I don't know, which I'm sure in a field this technical includes a lot. I delved a few layers deeper than John Oliver, but there's more below me than above. My political position on climate change, in other words, is built on a scaffolding of trust.

Admitting this, it's easy to see how climate change skepticism might be persuasive to some. According to a *Washington Post* and Kaiser Family Foundation poll from 2019, 20 percent of Americans do not believe human activity is causing the climate to change. Why do 20 percent of Americans side with fewer than 3 percent of scientists?* Politicization is one cause. Democrats are thirty percentage points more likely to believe humans are causing climate change, according to the same *WaPo*/Kaiser poll. As one party makes climate policy more central to their platform, it makes sense that the other party would grow resistant to it.

But there's a more fundamental reason for climate change skepticism: *the anxiety of knowing how little we ac-*

---

* Public opinion is moving fast on this issue. A Pew Research Center poll from back in 2016 found that *half* of Americans did not think human activity was driving climate change. A thirty-point shift in three years is extraordinary.

tually know. For all their accredited institutions, their rigorous processes and impact factors, scientists are essentially saying, *Trust us.* There's an unshakable feeling of vulnerability that comes with trust like that, in which a mass of knowledge is outsourced and remains obscure. The layperson can't confidently defend against challenges to the information contained within their trust, and that makes them susceptible to alternative theories, especially those that are equally technicalized. When faced with models and graphs claiming to show that climate change is not real, or not as bad as we think, or not caused by humans, the best response I have is an appeal to my trust in the experts, in the consensus.

Bad-faith actors exploit these insecurities. Those who stand to lose from action on climate change have marshaled considerable resources to hit us where we're vulnerable. They bankroll "studies" that dispute the consensus. They blitz the media with "experts" who question the findings, methods, and integrity of scientists. They donate heavily to politicians who lend credence to these dissenting narratives. There's a lot of power behind disinformation campaigns like this, a lot of money, but I don't think either would find a foothold if there weren't some lingering confusion in the minds of their targets. Fortunately, this attempt to muddy the discourse seems to be losing steam. As the latest polling shows, the public is rapidly approaching the same consensus as the experts.

But climate change is an easy case—not easy to solve, as our failure to take sufficient action proves again and again, but easy to judge. Earlier I asked: *When experts dis-*

agree, how do I decide? In the case of climate change, the experts do not disagree. They're virtually all on the same page regarding the basic facts, so it's easy for me to be on that page, too, and feel confident I've judged the issue correctly. Exactly where the issue falls in a list of priorities is up to every voter, but it's refreshing to have a clear sense of which direction to push. Such a settled debate is, unfortunately, rare in politics. Many other problems voters are asked to solve do not enjoy consensus among experts.

What then?

Take the minimum wage. There is an ongoing debate, which seems to be nearing its climax as I write this, about whether to raise the federal minimum wage to $15 an hour from its current $7.25. Democrats have made this increase a core plank of their party platform. Every major candidate for the Democratic nomination for president in 2020, except Andrew Yang, favored a $15 minimum wage. For several, it was a central campaign promise. In July 2019, the Democrat-led House of Representatives passed a bill to raise the minimum wage to $15 an hour, signaling the party's political will on the issue. (The bill promptly died in the Republican-led Senate, where it was not brought up for a vote.) On this issue, Democrats align with a majority of voters. According to 2019 polling from Pew, 67 percent of Americans "support raising the minimum wage to $15/hour, including 41% who say they strongly favor such an increase." The numbers are even more lopsided among Democrats and left-leaning Independents: 86 percent support the increase. Politicians looking for Democratic votes know which side of this debate to be on.

But what's the *right* thing to do?

What do the experts say?

Economics is the field that gives me the most uneasiness as a voter. That's not only because economies are vast and incredibly intricate; not only because my knowledge of their dynamics is tiny compared to all there is to know; not only because economic policies have huge impacts on people's lives; but because the economists themselves, the experts, have deep disagreements that I'm asked to adjudicate. On many questions there is no consensus to find, no overwhelming majority in which to place my trust. For a layperson, that can be a dizzying feeling, and a hard one to face. It has been for me. It's why people often start with the conclusion of their tribe and work backward to gather evidence for it, instead of starting with the evidence and using it to justify a conclusion. Sometimes that seems like the only way out of an impossible question.

Even if I wanted to construct a position the hard way, the ideological fracturing of the internet makes the backward approach more likely. When I click on *Vox*'s article "The Debate About the Minimum Wage, Explained," aren't I already entering a particular worldview, with assumptions that aren't necessarily shared by all reputable economists? AllSides.com, a website that rates the bias of online media organizations, labels *Vox* as Left on a spectrum of Left, Lean Left, Center, Lean Right, Right. There's no way to be exact with ratings like this, but AllSides's methodology, which draws on analyses from people across the political spectrum, seems thorough and legitimate. Another analysis, from Ad Fontes Media, finds bias in *Vox* content that "skews left." As a frequent reader of *Vox*, I broadly agree with these assessments. *Vox* promises to "explain the news," but I rarely see explainers on the benefits of right-wing ideas. This is probably because *Vox* explains and advocates for positions they believe to be evidently true, and do not seek balance for the sake of it. Biased doesn't necessarily mean wrong, of course, and I find most of the journalism on *Vox* to be reliable and insightful—yet I can't remember the last thing I read from them that really challenged my worldview, which also skews left.

That said, the article in question, "The Debate About the Minimum Wage, Explained" by Dylan Matthews, offers a good overview of the current research and disagreement in minimum wage studies. There may be some bias baked in, but I'm aware of it and on guard. And whether or not it's the best place to start, it's the place I *did* start in a good-faith attempt to understand the issue. It's what Google served me when I searched, "Should the United States raise the minimum wage to $15?"

When debating the merits of raising the minimum wage, the key question is whether or not it will cost jobs. As Matthews notes, a basic rule of economics is that "setting price floors—on milk, oil, or labor—causes supply to exceed demand." The critics of a minimum wage increase fear that employers will hire fewer people because they cost more money, or will reduce the hours of their existing employees for the same reason. They fear this lack of hiring and reduction in hours will outweigh the benefits of paying some workers higher wages. The *Vox* article focuses on a 2019 study by economist Arindrajit

Dube that found this fear largely unwarranted. The study was commissioned by the Conservative government of the United Kingdom, but was independently conducted by Dube, a professor of economics at the University of Massachusetts, Amherst.

The upshot from Dube's report was this: "Overall, the most up to date body of research from US, UK and other developed countries points to a very muted effect of minimum wages on employment, while significantly increasing the earnings of low paid workers." In fact, "the overall evidence base suggests an employment impact of close to zero."

Because this was a report for the UK, Dube naturally focused on that country's National Living Wage but he drew heavily from international research, too, including thirty-six estimates of minimum wage impact from the United States. Most minimum wage research comes from the United States, Dube noted, "because among developed countries, the US is somewhat unique in having a tremendous amount of variation in the effective minimum wages across localities, especially in recent years."

This is due to the fact that the federal minimum wage has remained flat in the last few decades (when adjusted for inflation), so several states and cities have taken matters into their own hands and exceeded the national standard. As a result, economists now have multiple examples of adjacent states and counties with different wage floors, ideal scenarios to study the consequences. Dube summarized the most recent US research in chapter 4 of his report, citing another 2019 study he was involved in. The upshot of that study is the same as the first: "The recent enactment of high minimum wages in US states have been absorbed with little loss in employment to date," even in states that have raised their minimum wages substantially, like California, Oregon, Washington, Colorado, Massachusetts, New York, and Maine, most of which are on a path to reach $12 or $15 an hour in the next few years. In other words, Dube believes that the greatest fear of proposed minimum wage hikes, that there will be significant negative employment effects, is not supported by the evidence.

Does this mean that Dube supports increasing the federal minimum wage to $15 an hour? Not exactly. Like any good economist, he knows there's some level at which a minimum wage *will* have negative effects. What's important to Dube is finding the limit at which there is a benefit to low-wage workers but minimal to no harmful effects to employment. Based on his research, Dube believes that "employment effects are small up to around 59% of the median wage," a number that varies widely across the United States. As of May 2020, the median hourly wage in San Francisco–Oakland–Hayward was $39.35—59 percent of that is $23.22. In the state of Alabama, the median was only $17.43—59 percent of that is $10.28. Implementing a $15 an hour minimum wage in Alabama would be setting it at 86 percent of the median, far beyond Dube's safe limit. This suggests that an across-the-board hike to $15 an hour could potentially prove harmful in some areas. To address this issue, Dube proposes a more tailored approach for state and local governments: set minimum wages to 50 percent of the local-area median wage, while factoring in the local prices of goods. After that, he would index minimum wages to inflation, protecting against real declines in the wage floor. This approach avoids some of the risks associated with a blanket hike at the federal level.

Though he may not be fully on board with the Fight for 15, Dube is an expert who wholeheartedly supports the minimum wage as a tool in the fight against poverty: "I find robust evidence that higher minimum wages lead to increases in incomes among families at the bottom of the income distribution and that these wages reduce the poverty rate." He believes that thoughtfully set minimum wages, increased over time, are a net benefit to the economy, and that a federal increase is long overdue.

Dube shares these sentiments with many other experts in the field, some of whom supported the congressional bill passed in 2019, which would have raised the federal minimum wage to $15 an hour by 2024. One of his colleagues, Michael Reich, a professor of economics at UC Berkeley, testified his endorsement of the bill to the House Education and Labor Committee: "A $15 minimum wage will generate a substantial economic stimulus because of the increased purchasing power for consumption." Reich went on to list some "beneficial downstream effects" he believed would result from the House bill, based on recent studies of minimum wage increases: "They reduce child neglect and poverty and improve child educational outcomes. They also reduce adult smoking rates, absenteeism from work for health reasons and obesity."

Dube and Reich don't speak for every economist on this issue, but they're far from outliers. They hold distinguished positions at prestigious institutions, and they've published work in reputable journals, cited by numerous colleagues. The same could be said for scores of economists who hold similar positions on this issue. Taken together, these experts represent an impressive amount of agreement about the positive effects of raising the minimum wage.

Agreement, but not consensus.

"While low wages contribute to the dire economic straits of many poor and low-income families, the argument that a higher minimum wage is an effective way to improve their economic circumstances is simply not supported by the evidence." That's from a 2018 paper by David Neumark, a professor of economics at UC Irvine. Neumark's work reflects a competing strain in minimum wage studies that paints a more pessimistic picture of these policies. In 2007, Neumark published a paper with William Wascher that found what critics of the minimum wage fear: "Among the papers we view as providing the most credible evidence, almost all point to negative employment effects." According to their review of the literature, raising the minimum wage *does* cost jobs. Even worse, Neumark and Wascher find "relatively overwhelming evidence" that the disemployment effects are felt most strongly in the least-skilled groups. The group that's supposed to be helped the most, they find, is actually hurt the worst.

It's been a while since 2007, but Neumark doesn't find the more recent work by Dube and his colleagues persuasive. In a 2014 response to a 2010 study by Dube, Neumark questioned his colleague's methodology. "The methods advocated in these studies," Neumark wrote, "do not isolate more reliable identifying information . . . and thus are flawed and lead to incorrect conclusions." Both sides have the same data, but they disagree on how to read it.

As I said before, economies are extraordinarily complex. Everything influences everything else. Isolating the effects of one factor, like the minimum wage, is devilishly hard. It makes sense that there would be debates on how best to do this. It makes sense that so many papers focus on what the other side failed to consider.

Like Dube and Reich, Neumark and his sympathetic colleagues hold distinguished positions at prestigious institutions, and they've published work in reputable journals, which is cited by their peers. It's clear that these disagreements are in good faith. Both sides are looking for the truth. They may advocate their positions with more confidence than is warranted, but that's what I expect from professionals presenting their life's work. I don't believe any of these experts have corrupt motives.

This doesn't mean there aren't any bad actors. The official-sounding Employment Policies Institute, for instance, publishes droves of material cataloging the supposed harms of raising the minimum wage. In researching this issue, I came across their work more than once, cited by those who oppose increases of any kind. After some digging, however, I discovered the EPI is owned by Berman and Company, a public relations firm that also represents the restaurant industry, which would be negatively affected by increases in the minimum wage. Their surveys, studies, and op-eds have the gloss of respectability, but the operation is tainted. According to the *New York Times*, Berman and Company "bills" the EPI for services its employees provide, effectively passing the donor money into the PR firm's coffers. (The EPI runs minimumwage .com, too, a polished website devoted to "Facts & Analysis." Beware.)

To be sure, the other side of the debate has its own monied interests, namely labor unions, who donate to think tanks like the Economic Policy Institute, another EPI. Though not as odious as Berman and Company, the Economic Policy Institute reliably publishes studies and surveys in favor of increases to the federal minimum wage—and those studies and surveys are reliably cited by activists with that policy goal.

Unfortunately, the minimum wage has become a partisan issue. In his *Vox* article, Matthews points to a dispiriting paper by researchers from Columbia Business School that finds a "robust correlation between patterns of academic writing and political behavior." If you know an economist's politics, in other words, you can predict their position on the minimum wage with unnerving accuracy. Partisanship like this makes people cynical and pessimistic. It's easy to question the trustworthiness of any expertise in a deeply polarized environment.

In this case, however, I believe there are real experts to find, experts trying to produce actionable knowledge that policymakers can use. They may come to the problem with different assumptions about what governments should do for people or how drastic the inequality problem really is, and that can color the world in different ways, but I believe they're sincerely trying to show us an objective picture of what the data say. In Neumark and Dube, I see honest experts with an honest disagreement.

That's the problem.

Putting my cards on the table, I'm a registered Democrat and believe the federal minimum wage should be increased. But can I say with *certainty* that this is the right thing to do? No, I can't. The best information I can gather on the question nudges me in one direction, but it isn't conclusive. Credible experts have divergent views. That's a stalemate I can't break, and as far as I can tell, neither can anyone else. Anybody speaking about this issue with complete conviction—from the president of the United States to your pal Gene from accounting—is either ignorant or dishonest. For the most part, I don't think the Genes of the world are bad people. If there's one thing I've learned from researching this, it's that it is *very easy* to find yourself in self-reinforcing parts of the internet, where whatever you click on seems to support what you've just been reading.

Partisan narratives can be very persuasive. Democrats often cite the shocking fact that, when adjusted for inflation, the current minimum wage is actually *lower* than it was in 1968. That just *feels* morally wrong, in the same way that it feels morally right to disallow profitable corporations from paying their workers a pittance.

On the other side, critics emphasize what everyone learns in Econ 101: setting price floors upsets the equilibrium of the economy. If a wage is set above what the market dictates, demand for labor will decrease, resulting in higher unemployment. Studies showing that minimum wage hikes don't follow this basic law are naturally treated with suspicion. Democrats' advocacy for a higher minimum wage fits nicely into a narrative on the right that paints left-wing voters as wanting to have their cake and eat it, too. Democrats, they think, like the *idea* of giving people more money, but fail to appreciate another fundamental rule of economics: there is no free lunch. This narrative isn't entirely unfounded, though Democrats are hardly the only party prone to oversimplifying.

So what do I do? When experts disagree, how do I decide? In debate club, we're taught that the side seeking change, the affirmative case, has the burden of proof. The negative case, the status quo, enjoys *presumption*. Affirmative debaters have to persuade a reasonable audience that their position is correct. Negative debaters don't need to defend the status quo, so much as rebut the narrative of the affirmative side. If they can prove that the affirmative argument is faulty or not entirely convincing, then they've done their job—the status quo wins out. This fits with a naturally cautious inclination in human beings. Trying something new always seems riskier than staying the course. The consequences of the latter might not be great, but at least they're known, while the consequences of the former are a bunch of big, scary question marks.

The more I read about economics, however, the more I see this line of thinking used as a cudgel against new ideas. Every time the minimum wage rises to the top of the national conversation, resistance is swift and stinks of fearmongering. At some point the status quo becomes an affirmative case of its own, a case against any change. Decades pass with no significant update to policies designed for a world long gone. The status quo becomes more and more entrenched, and the issue gets stuck in the mud of partisanship. After a while, staying the course may become more risky than trying something different.

As with climate science, there's a lot I don't know about economics, but I'm committed to learning more. It's every citizen's responsibility to be as informed as possible, and as someone fortunate enough to have a career devoted to learning new things, I have a greater responsibility than most. But I'll never be an expert on the minimum wage. I'll never be an economist or a climate scientist. In theory, I could pick one, maybe two specialties and commit my life to them. So could you. But that's not a practical solution to epistemic uncertainty. People have lives, jobs, families, bills. They have to take care of their aging parents, pick up groceries, do laundry, go to marriage counseling. The little leisure time they have, they deserve. If they want to play a pickup game of basketball on the weekend instead of reading a study about the downstream effects of the Affordable Care Act on socioeconomic disparities, who can blame them? I think there's time for personal lives *and* public responsibility, but there will never be enough time to escape our dependence on experts. That's a fact of life now, forever, and our dependency will only grow in the years to come, as the world becomes even more complex. We may reach consensus on some debates, as we have in climate science. On other questions experts will continue to disagree, and those questions will be on our ballots, too.

Much as I'd like a satisfactory answer to the question that prompted this essay, that's not why I wrote it. I already know the answer and it's unsatisfactory: when experts disagree, *I can't decide*. I wrote this essay to confront my limitations as a voter, and to confess an ignorance I'm still coming to terms with. I've learned a lot in the last decade, but feel less sure than ever. It's bad timing. The world pleads for good people to stand behind their beliefs.

"The best lack all conviction," Yeats wrote in "The Second Coming," "while the worst are full of passionate intensity." Those lines are usually interpreted as a comment on courage, or the lack of it, in times of fear and crisis. But what if the best lack conviction because conviction is impossible? What if the worst are the worst *because* they're passionately intense? I'm certainly not the best, and the people I hear in cafés who speak with certainty about the minimum wage—or nuclear energy, or foreign policy, or trade, or internet regulation—are probably not the worst. But I've become deeply skeptical of conviction in recent years, and much quieter at dinner parties as a result (at least when politics comes up).

That skepticism won't stop me from seeking conviction, but it won't stop the question from haunting me, either. It's true what Einstein said: "The more I learn, the more I realize how much I don't know." He's said to have said that, anyway. We don't really know for sure.

ESCAPE INTO MEANING

What in God's name drove me to watch the Lord of the Rings fifty times? It would be preposterous to watch any movie fifty times, but this is a trilogy, so it's triply preposterous, and each installment is more than three hours long (in the Extended Editions, which any fan of Peter Jackson's films will tell you are the *only* editions). That means I've spent something like six hundred hours watching the Lord of the Rings, which is twenty-five days or three and a half weeks, *almost a full month*. Jesus. Never did the math before.*

Most of those hours occurred in college. One night, my friend Sam and I put on *The Fellowship of the Ring* in his dorm and were mesmerized. We'd both seen it in theaters, both read the books, but were genuinely shocked by how well it held up on second viewing. The following nights we watched the remaining two films, then started from the

---

* The total run time of the Extended trilogy is 11 hours and 24 minutes. I rounded up a little in my calculation because, well, fifty viewings is probably an underestimate.

top a week later and did it again. We decided, sort of as an experiment, to continue watching the movies until we got bored with them, expecting that to happen after a couple more times through the trilogy.

A year later, we were still going.

Maybe our love of the halfling's leaf clouded our minds, but the magic just wouldn't die. Sam and I shared an apartment sophomore year, and when we both had a free night, we'd throw on one of the Extended Edition DVDs, whichever suited the mood. Those films are so long that they're split into two discs, so after a long day of classes one of us would yell into the hall: "One-two!" or "Three-one!" First number for film, second for disc. I usually chose 1-1, *Fellowship* through the Council of Elrond (I'm a sucker for the Shire and anything with Ian Holm as Bilbo) or 2-1, the first part of *The Two Towers*, which has the introduction of Rohan and my favorite scene in the trilogy: King Théoden mourning his son's passing, holding the simbelmynë flower. ("Ever has it grown on the tombs of my forebears. Now it shall cover the grave of my son.") But I could be persuaded to watch any disc, given the right argument.

Eventually, after far more rewatches than either of us anticipated, after Sam and I could perform the entire saga by heart, after Gandalf launched a thousand fireworks and Boromir was pierced with a thousand arrows, after a million orcs sieged Helm's Deep and dozens of rings were cast back into the fiery chasms whence they came, the thrill finally faded.

For a while, anyway. Since that feverish year, I've revisited the movies periodically, a few times for Nerdwriter videos, but mostly as comfort food. A few months ago, during COVID lockdown, I watched the trilogy with my wife, who had never seen it before. It was like having fresh eyes. I tried not to be that guy who pauses the movie to say things like "When Aragorn kicked that helmet, Viggo Mortensen actually broke his foot, but still managed to stay in character!" My wife is not really a science fiction/ fantasy fan, so it was fun to see her get drawn into the story. Recently, I've taken to watching LOTR "first reaction" videos on YouTube, which are exactly what they sound like: someone who's never seen the movies records themselves reacting to key moments. These kinds of videos have multiplied during the pandemic, earning hundreds of thousands of views. Guess I'm not the only Tolkien junkie trying to recapture the high of that first fix.

It started with the films but didn't end there. I've read the books a few times now, as well as *The Silmarillion*, *Unfinished Tales*, *The Children of Húrin*, and *The Hobbit*. I've pored through Tolkien's letters, read his essays, watched all the extant footage of him, listened to every radio interview. I've even written some LOTR fan poetry, a few verses that were mercifully lost when an old laptop died out of embarrassment. These things don't put me in the upper ranks of Tolkien superfandom— just ask Stephen Colbert or the people who can actually speak Elvish—but I've spent a not insignificant amount of my life in the world he built. And it still pulls at me, still mesmerizes. It's appropriate to meet great art with great enthusiasm, but I think we can all agree that this is . . . something else.

As you saw in my essay about cyberpunk, I have a proclivity for certain kinds of escapist art. In *Blade Runner* and cyberpunk novels, I found an escape from the responsibilities of relationships, from the labels others place on us, and from the fragmenting pressures of modern culture, in which individuals must fend for themselves in dizzying crosscurrents of meaning. Cyberpunk is a space that affirms the essential meaninglessness of all things, a fantasy zone where it's no longer necessary to work at finding a place in the world. You're given permission to let go, to let the slipstream carry you where it will, through dazzling neon cityscapes pulsing with the music of Vangelis.

I'm beginning to realize that Middle-earth serves an opposite function. If cyberpunk is an escape from meaning, a surrender to reality at its most nihilistic, then the Lord of the Rings is an escape *into* meaning, a longing for reality as I want it to be. If nothing has a purpose in the Sprawl, *everything* has a purpose in Middle-earth. Every person is circumscribed by their role in the mythology. There are prophecies, objects of sacred value, destinies even for hobbits. As Gandalf tells Frodo in the Mines of Moria, "Bilbo was meant to find the Ring. In which case, you were also meant to have it. And that is an encouraging thought." It would be encouraging to know that you were *meant* to do something, but unfortunately I don't think that's the case in our world.

I'm betraying my beliefs, so let me put them on the table: I don't think there is any objective purpose for humanity, or that there is a god of any kind. I don't believe people have destinies. I think everything that's happened since the Big Bang has happened by accident, following from physical laws that are inherently meaningless, like our lives.

That's a bummer of a personal philosophy, I know. But I'm not denying *all* meaning, only the meaning that most religions believe comes from on high, the kind Gandalf sees in Frodo. What undoubtedly does exist is the meaning we give to things, personally and collectively. Subjective meanings can be as fulfilling as the ones people turn to God for, but you have to choose them and the choosing can be hard. I'm not trying to change minds. I have no issue with believers. Often, I envy them.

I see the appeal of divine purpose. Much as I pat myself on the back for a stoic refusal to succumb to magical thinking, I can't deny that something at the core of me longs for Meaning with a capital M. It feels ancient, biological. For philosopher and author Albert Camus, this longing is the essence of the Absurd: the existential conflict between beings who are disposed to look for the Meaning of Life and a universe that can't provide it.

I first read Camus's essay "The Myth of Sisyphus" in my twenties, and it was like seeing a transcript of my thoughts.* "That nostalgia for unity," writes Camus, "that appetite for the absolute illustrates the essential impulse of the human drama." The impulse for meaning is baked into us, and we can't rid ourselves of it, no matter how squarely we face "the unreasonable silence of the world." According to Camus, all we can do is accept the absurdity of our situation, refuse false consolations like religion, and move on

---

* Sound familiar?

with the difficult but eventually rewarding work of making meaning for ourselves.

Easier said than done. Our "appetite for the absolute" is always seeking outlets. The Lord of the Rings is one for me. Tolkien's mythology imagines a world in which there *is* a design to creation, in which supernatural things *do* happen. To the extent that the story is immersive, the reader can participate in this alternate universe, escape into its meanings, without having to believe something untrue. That's because the participation is literary, not actual. It's sort of like a loophole: in art, you can indulge in the consolations reason denies in life.

Tolkien's Middle-earth is the ideal place for this kind of indulgence. It's impossible to imagine a more detailed "Secondary World," as he called it. The maps, the languages, the lineages, the lore—Middle-earth is a staggering feat of worldbuilding. Its density rewards exploration, enlivening every corner of the stories that take place there. That the Lord of the Rings does not suffer for Tolkien's fanatic landscaping is a testament to his skill as a storyteller—but that doesn't make it any less fanatical. Even before the movies visualized it, Middle-earth was a place you could see with perfect clarity. Here's Gimli's description of the Glittering Caves tucked behind Helm's Deep:

Gems and crystals and veins of precious ore glint in the polished walls; and the light glows through folded marbles, shell-like, translucent as the living hands of Queen Galadriel. There are columns of white and saffron and dawn-rose, Legolas, fluted and twisted into dreamlike forms; they spring up from many-colored floors to meet the glistening pendants of the roof: wings, ropes, curtains fine as frozen clouds; spears, banners, pinnacles of suspended palaces!

The brief depiction of these caves in the film is a pale rendering of Tolkien's prose. But that's not a knock on Peter Jackson. The movies did a stunning job of bringing Middle-earth to life, but no movie, no trilogy, not even one with a combined budget of $281 million, could approach the intricacy of Tolkien's vision. We're talking about an epic tale of good and evil in which the prologue contains an entire section about the varieties and customs of pipe-weed in different regions of the Shire!

Tolkien couldn't resist. He detailed his imaginary world with obsessive passion. But the obsession didn't start with Middle-earth—believe it or not, that was a by-product. For Tolkien, everything always started with language.

Some teens experiment with drugs. Tolkien experimented with invented languages. The earliest was Animalic, a language fabricated by his cousins out of animal names. He was never fluent in it, but recalled to a prestigious literary society at Oxford that "dog nightingale woodpecker forty" meant "you are an ass." Next came Nevbosh, also created by a cousin but more complex, then Naffarin, which was his own. Constructing new languages was Tolkien's "secret vice," and even after he made the study of *real* languages his career as a philologist and professor of

Anglo-Saxon at Oxford, he continued to do it, enchanted by the beauty of words.

As his own languages grew more sophisticated, he realized that "for the perfect construction of an art-language it is found necessary to construct at least in outline a mythology" to go with it. "Your language construction will breed a mythology." Maybe you can see where this is going. If not, here's an excerpt from a letter Tolkien wrote to the Houghton Mifflin Company, after the publication of the Lord of the Rings, which drives the point home:

> The invention of languages is the foundation [of *The Lord of the Rings* and other tales of Middle-earth]. The "stories" were made rather to provide a world for the languages than the reverse. To me a name comes first and the story follows . . . [*The Lord of the Rings*] is to me, anyway, largely an essay in "linguistic aesthetic," as I sometimes say to people who ask me "what is it all about?"

If Middle-earth feels many times more solid than most fantasy worlds, this is why. At its core is language, the seed from which its mythology grows. Tolkien searched his languages for the stories they contained, and would have written the Lord of the Rings in Elvish if given the choice. (Many millions of fans are glad he didn't.) Even in English, the history and environment of Middle-earth feel discovered rather than invented. It's so real you half expect an archaeologist to stumble across a Gondorian helmet in the English countryside.

For the keen escapist, Middle-earth is the premier destination. It never breaks the illusion. Every river and ruin, every poem and sword, every place the Fellowship alights on its journey through the story can be traced back ages to the earliest days of the world—and even before that, to the moment of divine creation by Eru Ilúvatar, the supreme being of this universe. It's all infused with a feeling of deep history, and the effect of that on the reader (at least the effect on *this* reader) is overwhelmingly immersive.

Does a story need to have such detail to be immersive? Of course not. You can fashion a world from a handful of words. But the immersion Middle-earth triggers is more extreme. It's a world that exists independently of the story. At any point you could break away from the hobbits, head north, and wander the abandoned fortress at Deadman's Dike, which was once called Norbury, or Fornost, former capital of Arthedain, ruled by Amlaith, son of Eärendur, and his Dúnedain descendants, until it fell to the Witch King of Angmar in the year 1974 of the Third Age, after which—well, you get the idea.

Importantly, this immersion is not a "suspension of disbelief." Tolkien cringed at the phrase. "What really happens," he explains in "On Fairy-Stories," "is that the story-maker proves a successful 'sub-creator.' [The writer] makes a Secondary World which [the reader's] mind can enter. Inside it, what [the writer] relates is 'true': it accords with the laws of that world. You therefore believe it, while you are, as it were, inside."

This belief is similar in feeling, but not in substance, to the belief we experience in the real world. It's Secondary

Belief for a Secondary World, less like persuasion than enchantment. "Enchantment," Tolkien writes, "produces a Secondary World into which both designer and spectator can enter, to the satisfaction of their senses while they are inside; but in its purity it is artistic in desire and purpose." When you're inside the fantasy world, you believe in things that aren't true. You believe in magic rings or invisibility cloaks or alchemy, but these Secondary Beliefs don't cross over to the real world. In the real world, we hold Primary Beliefs.

I have plenty of Primary Beliefs, for which I have varying degrees of evidence. Beliefs about politics, how to treat others, the best movies ever made. Beliefs relying on my trust in smart people, like my belief in the dangers of climate change. I believe, based on the vast number of galaxies, that there *is* intelligent life elsewhere in the universe (though I don't believe they've been here). I believe my friends and family care for me. I believe the stock market will rise in the long term. I believe everything tastes better with Valentina hot sauce.

But I don't believe in the supernatural—ghosts or magic or witchcraft or gods. These are not included in my Primary Beliefs, or they *are* included, just in a negative sense: I believe that there has never been a supernatural occurrence. I believe there is no such thing as ghosts, magic, etc. Again, these things are personal, and I'm not trying to proselytize. What interests me isn't so much the beliefs (or unbeliefs) themselves, but that as a consequence of having them, I'm blocked from a certain type of shared experience, one that is deeply profound to those who feel it: *the experience of the holy*.

Maybe a little etymology is in order. Tolkien the philologist would love that.

"Holy" comes from the Old English *hālig*, meaning "consecrated, sacred, godly, ecclesiastical," which is derived from *hāl*, "whole, uninjured, complete, entire, health." This, in turn, comes from the Proto-Germanic *hailagaz*, which again means "sacred," and further back from the Proto-Indo-European root *kailo* for "whole, uninjured." In its use today, "holy" implies a connection to divinity, drawing on a sense of wholeness found in its roots—like the unity Camus believes we're predisposed to desire. As I understand it, the experience of the holy is not the same as feelings of wonder or awe or oneness, which can be evoked by anything.

Here's an example of the difference:

I love the Gothic architecture you find across Europe. Years ago, I lived in a suburb north of Paris called Saint-Denis, home to the Basilique cathédrale de Saint-Denis, known as the first ever Gothic structure. On free afternoons, I'd walk there from my apartment, find an empty pew, and sit for a while. The place is breathtaking: cross-ribbed vaulted arches lead down the nave to the Rayonnant choir, lined with stained glass. High on the transept walls, rosette windows like colossal violet eyes stare at each other, filling the space with light. Even the ambulatory is light-filled, thanks to Abbot Suger's innovative design. I'd head over there, admiring the radiating chapels, before making my way to the tombs where every French king from the tenth century to the eighteenth rests beneath his effigy. Except for the shuffle of feet and the occasional whisper, the place was always silent. No other kind of public space is like this. It's a silence centuries old, a silence that kindles reflection. I felt a deep reverence there, and awe.

But I didn't feel the holy. What I experienced was qualitatively different, I think, from what Catholics feel in the Basilique cathédrale de Saint-Denis at Sunday Mass. The beauty of the structure may move them, too, but it's augmented by their belief in the divinity that resides there. It's linked to God, to salvation, to the ultimate destiny of humanity in which they play a meaningful role.

Several thinkers have attempted to analyze this religious experience, from Freud to William James to Rudolf Otto, who coined the term "numinous" to do so. According to Otto, the numinous is a sense of mystery both terrifying and fascinating. It can pass over you suddenly like a "gentle tide, pervading the mind with a tranquil mood of deepest worship." Or it may "burst in sudden eruption up from the depth of the soul with spasms and convulsions." The best description of the numinous belongs not to Otto, but to C. S. Lewis, a friend of Tolkien:

Suppose you were told there was a tiger in the next room: you would know that you were in danger and would probably feel fear. But if you were told "There is a ghost in the next room," and believed it, you would feel, indeed, what is often called fear, but of a different kind. It would not be based on the knowledge of danger, for no one is primarily afraid of what a ghost may do to him, but of the mere fact that it is a ghost. It is "uncanny" rather than dangerous, and the special kind of fear it excites may be called Dread. With the Uncanny one has reached the fringes of the Numinous. Now suppose that you were told simply "There is a mighty spirit in the room," and believed it. Your feelings would then be even less like the mere fear of danger: but the disturbance would be profound. You would feel wonder and a certain shrinking—a sense of inadequacy to cope with such a visitant and of prostration before it.

The key thing there is "and believed it." The numinous, the experience of the holy, is a response to a genuine belief in supernatural things. In recent years, some have tried to reclaim the numinous for certain intense secular experiences, like awe or oneness with nature or the kaleidoscopic adventures of psychedelic drugs. I've tried those drugs and felt the "ego dissolution" Michael Pollan describes in *How to Change Your Mind*. It's a profound sensation, but I wouldn't call it numinous.

At least not as I interpret it. The missing piece isn't the feeling of unity. I feel that on occasion, like everyone. I felt it in the Basilique cathédrale de Saint-Denis, on a bench last Tuesday, in sixth grade when Mrs. Entenmann told us the atoms in our bodies come from the insides of faraway stars. What's missing is the conviction that the unity *means* something, that I being part of it have some role relative to its greater purpose. I don't have that conviction.

In *this* world, anyway.

In the Secondary World, you're not bound by Primary Beliefs. "There are ancient limitations from which fairy-stories offer a sort of escape," says Tolkien, "and old ambitions and desires . . . to which they offer a kind of satisfaction and consolation." These desires are many, and Tolkien names a few: the desire to swim in the deeps of the sea, to fly unaided in clear skies, to converse with animals, to escape from death like the elves of Middle-earth. But the highest consolation of the fairy story, according to Tolkien, is the Happy Ending, "the sudden joyous turn," which arrives just as everything seems hopeless, "giving a fleeting glimpse of Joy, Joy beyond the walls of the world, poignant as grief." It is the Happy Ending that gives the rest of the narrative its meaning, that assigns significance to characters and events. At this moment of "miraculous grace," everything is suddenly linked in a chain of perfect causality. Everyone is suddenly stamped with purpose.

In his book *Nature and the Numinous in Mythopoeic Fantasy Literature*, Chris Brawley explores the connection between Tolkien's position on fairy stories and Otto's concept of the numinous. Brawley argues that the numinous we encounter in fairy stories (via Secondary Belief) enables us to "revise our perceptions of the natural world." We bring those feelings *back into the primary world*, in other words, and they have the power to "re-sacrilize" nature, to restore holiness to our experience of it. Because of this, Brawley says, fantasy literature, and especially the Lord of the Rings, offers a potent environmental message.

"This renewed relationship with the natural world," Brawley writes, "seeks to view nature as a part of a community, not a commodity." There's no doubt Tolkien would endorse this. He had an abiding love for the environment and a disdain for man's attempts to dominate it. "In all my works," he once wrote to a newspaper, "I take the part of trees as against all their enemies."

Brawley's marvelous book, like Tolkien's "On Fairy-Stories," defends fantasy against negative connotations of escapism. The criticism most often hurled at "escapist" art is that it offers a comforting and simplistic alternate reality in which people can avoid engaging with the real world in all its complexity. Escapism exists in many forms—advertising, for example, is the escapist medium par excellence—but fantasy often bears the brunt of these aspersions. I think that's down to three things:

1. fantasy's proximity to fairy tales, which we mistakenly associate only with kids;
2. the use of magic and the supernatural;
3. the powerful immersion Secondary Worlds can trigger.

Brawley and Tolkien do a persuasive job showing that this criticism is itself reductive, and I'm sympathetic to their arguments. I'm also sympathetic to some of the criticisms. Escapism *can* be troubling in certain contexts, especially when it grips large groups.

"I thought it was a really worrying sign," comics icon Alan Moore said recently about superhero films, "that hundreds of thousands of adults were queuing up to see characters that were created fifty years ago to entertain twelve-year-old boys. That seemed to speak to some kind of longing to escape the complexities of the modern world, and go back to a nostalgic, remembered childhood."

As someone who's been a comics fan for years, who's defended their worth, who's waited in those queues, I can't deny his point. We all use entertainment to escape the world. Given the state of it, can you blame us? The question isn't whether people use art to escape; it's whether we use it too much. Alan Moore seems to believe we do. Others are more forgiving. All I know for sure is that I shouldn't be the one to draw the line.

Because I *do* use the Lord of the Rings as a comforting, simplistic fantasy. It's true that Tolkien inspires me to look at the natural world anew, like Brawley suggests, and that influences my actions toward the environment, but this isn't the major draw of his work for me. The major draw is its satisfaction of Camus's "nostalgia for unity." The numinous I encounter there emanates from a universe that's *actually* designed. That design speaks through objects that are *actually* sacred, figures who are *actually* holy. Gandalf, for example, is a Maia, a lesser angel of Tolkien's cosmology, sent into Middle-earth to aid its peoples in their fight against Sauron, another Maia and the primary villain of the Lord of the Rings. Gandalf's mission is ordained by the Valar, divine beings who helped shape the world through the music of Eru Ilúvatar, the omnipotent deity. The clash between Gandalf and Sauron, between the forces of good and evil, is

Written—in the larger sense of God's Plan, but also in the sense that Tolkien wrote it.

But these two things are effectively the same: it's *story* that bestows meaning.

That's the comforting fantasy. When I say simplistic, I obviously don't mean Tolkien's vision for Middle-earth is simple. For Eru's sake, everything has multiple names in multiple invented languages! But any story, even one as dense and detailed as the Lord of the Rings, is necessarily simpler than reality. Any universe that's designed, that has a Designer—whether an omnipotent god or an Oxford don—is necessarily a reductive version of our own. By virtue of having an ending, happy or not, stories impose order on disordered existence. Some fictions minimize order to better reflect reality as it is. Others are content to order tiny slivers of reality, those places and times in which the story takes place. Fantasy of Tolkien's variety is much more brazen. It strives to construct a fully realized Secondary World, in which everything is accounted for—if not by description, then by implication. When this is done well, the reader becomes immersed to the point of Secondary Belief in a story that feels as immense as reality yet saturated with meaning. For the duration of that escape, it's as if you really are part of a cosmic tale.

This is why—I'm realizing as I write this—the Lord of the Rings never gets boring for me. The first time through you see the plot, the twists and turns, and that's exciting. But the second time, when you know how it all turns out, you see the meaning. The first time, you see how Gandalf's death and Boromir's betrayal lead

Frodo to break from the Fellowship. The second time, you see Frodo's parting *in* Gandalf's death, *in* Boromir's betrayal. Each moment contains its consequences. What you're watching isn't so much a story unfolding as destiny being fulfilled.

A cosmic destiny: with Tolkien's world being so rich, the meanings of events in the Lord of the Rings aren't relevant just to the few years it covers, but to the many thousands of years in the larger mythology. The immortal elves testify to that, characters like Elrond and Galadriel, who have lived in Middle-earth for Ages and witnessed the arc of fate. As the story becomes more familiar, as you absorb the nuances of Tolkien's creation, that sensation of meaning grows. And if the numinous is what you're there for, rereads and rewatches become more gratifying, not less. You get to a point where holiness invigorates everything, like a dazzling inner glow.

Tolkien was a devout Roman Catholic, and the numinous he conjures in Middle-earth, that "fleeting glimpse of Joy," was for him a window into the real numinous, the actual holiness of God. He believed that the reason we create Secondary Worlds is "because we are made: and not only made, but made in the image and likeness of a Maker." For Tolkien, the story of Christ is a fairy story "that has entered history and the primary world." The joy we experience upon learning this is "exactly the same quality, if not the same degree, as the joy which the 'turn' in a fairy-story gives: such joy has the very taste of primary truth." The Christian can rejoice in the fact that "his bents and faculties have a purpose, which can be redeemed."

All this, I disagree with. I also disagree with Tolkien when he says of Christianity, "There is no tale ever told that men would rather find was true," and "to reject it leads either to sadness or to wrath."

I don't wish that the Christian story—or the Jewish story I learned growing up, or any story that invokes the supernatural—were true. And I certainly don't believe rejecting it leads to sadness or wrath. You can be happy and kind making meaning for yourself. Millions do it every day. As I said in my essay about cyberpunk, escapist fantasies are laughably superficial. Attaining them isn't what we really want. If we did, they'd no doubt bore or disappoint us. We don't want the fantasy. We want to fantasize.

My obsession with the Lord of the Rings, what drove me to watch it fifty times (so far), doesn't speak to a secret desire for religion, but to a peculiar feature of the human mind: its craving for meaning. The mind searches for and finds that meaning in stories. The bigger the story, the greater the meaning. It casts about for the tale that incorporates everything, but reality can't oblige, so it settles for smaller stories, conditional stories, stories it creates. Still, an appetite for the Big One lingers. You can't shake off what your mind is predisposed to want. You can't indulge it, either, not in the real world, not without changing your beliefs. But there's another way, through a magical side door carved with ancient runes that opens at the right Elvish word onto a strange and significant country . . .

ODE TO PUBLIC BENCHES

I can't see their faces anymore—only their eyes, what they're wearing, what they're carrying. An elderly woman pinches her husband's jacket behind the elbow; somehow it's more intimate than locking arms or holding hands. He's carrying a translucent *fruteria* bag, through which I can see green apples, cherries, and a sweet potato. Passing them on the left, a trio of young women laugh at something on a phone. They're speaking German. Tourists? If so, they're the first I've seen in months. On a warm April day in any other year, Rambla de Catalunya would be swarming. The café terraces on the pedestrian mall would be full; people would hover nearby, waiting for a table to open. Today, the street is livelier than it's been in a while, but bare compared to the pre-pandemic normal. Across from me, a small group of colleagues consult paperwork at Forn de Sant Jaume, drinking Estrellas that look irresistible in the sun. The cries of monk parakeets draw my attention to the building on the opposite side of the street. It's gorgeous. I enter the address into my phone and learn that it's Casa Fargas, designed in 1904 by Enric Sagnier, an elegant example of the Catalan Modernism that typifies this neighborhood. Balconies to the left and right echo a curve in the central tribune, so the facade looks like a gentle wave. A little girl nearly runs over my foot with her scooter. I flinch. It still startles me when strangers get close. I wonder when that will pass, *if* it will pass. I smile at her mother, but I'm not sure she can tell with my face behind the mask. A breeze picks up and rustles the plane trees, triggering a feeling of perfect loveliness. I am absorbed into the scene I'd been observing. Ten or maybe thirty minutes later, I rise from the bench and head home.

This is an ode to public benches, those vital but often invisible staples of urban design. I've had more moments of genuine peace on public benches than anywhere else, that inner quiet you recognize as it's happening, that feeling of oneness with your surroundings. Usually, my surroundings are urban. I've had great times on country and suburban benches, but most of my life happens in cities, and most of my benches are city benches. I'm in Barcelona as I write this, where I've been living since COVID-19 closed the world. I planned this essay well before the pandemic, but this year has increased my appreciation for public benches in ways I couldn't have anticipated. For much of 2020, sitting on a bench was basically *all you could do* in Barcelona (and every other city). Resources became lifelines, an escape from the walls of our apartments. Benches became front-row seats to the postapocalyptic displays of empty city centers.

In "normal" times, benches are an escape of a different sort, an escape from the relentless flow of metropolitan
streets. For the most part, cities encourage you to move
from point A to point B without pause. That's what the
majority of city dwellers are doing outside—heading to
work, to the store, the gym, a restaurant, heading home. If
you *do* pause in New York City, for example, where I lived
some years ago, you run the risk of being trampled by the
herd. The bench allows you to step away from that herd. It
transforms the surroundings into a place to be, instead of
just a place to pass through. The simple act of sitting radically alters your relationship to the city, and to the people
you share it with. And benches are radical in another way:
like public parks where you find lots of them, benches don't
require consumption, unlike almost all other destinations
in a city. Small as a bench may seem, it's an important part
of the "urban commons": spaces and services shared, used,
and controlled by citizens, not market forces.

City benches are also the best places on earth to people-
watch, one of my favorite pastimes. The parade of humanity
is endlessly fascinating, and from the bench you can watch
it with the special anonymity cities provide. In my essay on
cyberpunk, I wrote about the liberating feeling of disap-
pearing into a metropolis. Under that invisibility cloak, you
can really *see* others—without being preoccupied by their
perception of you, or what you think their perception is.
Maybe I'm overly self-conscious (I definitely am), but my
mind is too busy during social interactions to observe the
people I'm interacting with. Mostly I'm just trying to make
it through the conversation without embarrassing myself.

There's a tranquility to people-watching I rarely have when socializing. Public benches disappear into the background with whomever is on them, and in that camouflage the bothersome ego can disappear, too.

To draw on ideas from earlier in this book, people-watching on city benches is like Baudelaire's flâneur combined with Emerson's "transparent eyeball."

A flâneur is an urban wanderer who delights in spectating the diverse metropolitan crowds, a type that first appeared in nineteenth-century Paris, around the time when Baron Haussmann reshaped the city. The word comes from *flânerie*, referring to the act of idly strolling, wasting time. Flâneurs like Baudelaire meandered through the streets, alleys, and glass-roofed arcades of Paris, partaking in what Balzac called "the gastronomy of the eye." On a bench, you become a *stationary* flâneur (something of a contradiction in terms). Instead of strolling through the world, the world strolls by you.

For Baudelaire, the flâneur was both observer and participant, detached from the crowd in one moment, subsumed in it the next. These alternating roles are what I cherish about my experiences on city benches. It usually happens in the way I described in the first paragraph: I start by observing, people-watching, letting my focus drift over the scene without purpose, like a flâneur drifts through the city. Then something happens, something trivial—a shaft of light strikes between two awnings and picks out a pyramid of oranges, or wind rustles the plane trees—and I *dissolve* into the world. No longer a spectator, I give myself over to the spectacle.

This is the feeling that reminds me of Emerson's "transparent eyeball," a metaphor he created to describe an act of observing that goes beyond mere looking:

> Crossing a bare common, in snow puddles, at twilight, under a clouded sky, without having in my thoughts any occurrence of special good fortune, I have enjoyed a perfect exhilaration. I am glad to the brink of fear. . . . Standing on the bare ground,— my head bathed by the blithe air and uplifted into infinite space,—all mean egotism vanishes. I become a transparent eye-ball; I am nothing; I see all.

As I said in my essay about him, Emerson has a magical way of reaching up centuries to perfectly articulate what you're feeling. This captures my experiences on public benches exactly. Emerson found divinity in nature, and his way of communing with it was visual. He tells us to go into nature and *see*, to examine its "manifold natural objects" and let their beauty imprint on the mind. In doing so, "all mean egotism vanishes" and you're assimilated into the harmony that exists behind the forms of the world.

Though Emerson invokes God, I don't think there's anything mystical about this philosophy. There *is* a link between all things in the universe. At the most basic level, we're made of the same stuff as sand, skyscrapers, and stars. Our feelings of separateness—from nature and from one another—are accidents of perception and psychology. It's possible for brief moments to see beyond this evolutionary programming, to experience harmony with what's outside yourself. We all have moments like this. Emerson had them walking across a Concord commons.

I have them on city benches.

The view from Rambla de Catalunya may not be the one Emerson had in mind, but the city offers its own beauty, just as it offers its own solitude. Emerson preferred country life over the "artificial and curtailed life of cities." Here, I'm more in tune with Baudelaire and the flâneurs, who appreciated the pageant of the metropolis. Take the transparent eyeball, transport it to the city center. Take the strolling flâneur, seat him on the bench. Sounds like a perfect afternoon to me—and it doesn't cost a dime!

As Samuel Beckett wrote, "We spend our life, it's ours, trying to bring together in the same instant a ray of sunshine and a free bench."

Of course, you don't need a transcendent, this-is-where-I-fit-in-the-cosmos experience for a bench to have value. You could just be tired or need somewhere to tie your shoes. You could be feeling cooped up and desperate to get out of the house. You don't want to eat. You don't want to shop. You don't want to pay $4.50 for a coffee just so you can sit at the corner café. But the parklet at the end of the block has a few benches—that'll do the trick. Yesterday, I was having one of those bad writing days when your mind tries to convince you that everything you've ever written is dogshit because you are dogshit in the shape of a human being. You know, a typical Tuesday. So I took a walk and found a nearby bench to clear my head. There's no getting rid of your inner jerk, but the most effective way to shut him up, I've found, is to go outside.

Public benches, like public parks, are more than just nice-to-have resources. In urban centers, they're essential for maintaining public health. Being outside destresses, boosts vitamin D, reduces blood pressure, improves mood, sleep, even memory. A 2019 study from the *International Journal of Environmental Health Research* shows that spending just twenty minutes in a public park increases life satisfaction, even if you don't exercise while you're there. People *need* to be outside, and they deserve to have outdoor spaces that are free and easy to access, spaces where they can linger for a while and feel welcome.

These spaces foster the health of the community as much as the health of individuals. They promote a sense of belonging, and when people feel like they belong, they invest more energy into the community. They're also important sites of socialization, often between individuals or groups that might not otherwise interact. Simply sharing the same physical space, seeing and being seen, amplifies empathy across social divides. We know that the city can be an isolating place. A shared bench can make it feel less so.

This idea of public spaces being a site for socializing and discourse has long represented an ideal of city life— going back at least as far as the ancient Greeks[*]—and it remains a goal of modern urban planning. Public space is considered successful when it attracts individuals and

---

[*] In *Ten Books on Architecture* (30–15 BCE), the Roman architect Vitruvius writes about the ancient Greek palaestra, a public wrestling school that consisted of an open-air rectangular court surrounded by colonnades. Though it was traditionally used for wrestling and other sporting events, the palaestra also served as a place for socialization and debate. "In the three colonnades construct roomy recesses with seats in them," he advises, "where philosophers, rhetoricians, and others who delight in learning may sit and converse."

groups to socialize there, and nothing attracts better than seating.

"The most popular plazas tend to have considerably more sitting space than less well-used ones," writes William Whyte in his classic 1980 book *The Social Life of Small Urban Spaces*. Whyte and a team of researchers observed several plazas in New York City to determine why some are routinely congested, while others remain empty. A major factor, which he concedes is no "intellectual bombshell," is the availability of seating. "The most attractive fountains, the most striking designs cannot induce people to come and sit if there is no place to sit." That may be obvious, Whyte notes, but we often miss the obvious, as several seat-starved plazas prove.

When Whyte says "seating," he's not necessarily talking about the classic bench you probably picture in your mind—the iron and green-painted wood Central Park settee. Public seating can be anything from a building ledge to a fountain rim to stairs. Whyte mocks classic benches as "artifacts the purpose of which is to punctuate architectural photographs." He can't deny their superior comfort—backrests and armrests are a nice bonus—but laments that they're too often situated poorly in the space, discouraging socializing. What's worse, planners frequently freeze benches in "concrete permanence." We ought to allow for experimentation, he says, time to observe which benches people choose and which they don't, "but rarely will you ever see a plan for a public space that even countenances the possibility that parts of it might not work very well." Alas, many fine benches go butt-less.

This is an ode to public benches, but it might have been titled "An Ode to Public Seating." What I love about benches applies to all the seats Whyte lists. I'm not picky. A slab of concrete works for me. So do planter ledges, of which there are many on the Boston University campus (where I attended school). I love the green SENAT chairs that pepper the Paris parks, which you can arrange in any configuration. I've lounged happily on the Low Memorial Library steps at Columbia (where I did not attend school), what students call the "concrete beach." Downtown from Columbia, at the High Line, an elevated park on a former railroad spur, designers listened to Whyte's obvious advice and made sure there are plenty of places to sit: a radial bench curves along the path at Twenty-Ninth and Thirtieth Streets; at Twenty-Third, steps of reclaimed teak wood rise up against a brick facade; and on the sun deck at Fourteenth Street, wooden chaise lounges slide along the original rail track, a stylish medium between full movability and "concrete permanence."

But my favorite place to sit is Venice, Italy, where I had the good luck to live for a couple of months in 2016. The stone banks of its canals, the steps of its churches and foot bridges, are perfect places to while the hours away. Legs dangling over a canal, watching water taxis pass below a fifteenth-century church of colored marble—that's some world-class public seating. Eat your heart out, bench.

Ample seating boosts socializing in all its forms. On city benches I mostly people-watch, what Clare Cooper Marcus calls "covert socializing." If I gather with strangers to listen to a street musician, or meet my friends for a picnic in the park, that's "overt socializing." For a public space to achieve its highest potential, it should enable both types. Covert socializing is the easiest to instigate with good design, followed by overt socializing among friends. More difficult to pull off is overt socializing among strangers, especially those of different backgrounds, yet this is the kind that yields the most upside to community health.

So what can we do to encourage it?

In *Life Between Buildings*, the Danish architect Jan Gehl discovered another obvious but underappreciated truth: to achieve a variety of interactions, you need to get lots of people in the same place. Fortunately, this is what human beings like, even if they say otherwise. In his study, Whyte learned that individuals instinctively congregate—they "self-congest"—despite *saying* they want space and escape from others. As a result of this confusion, many urban spaces are designed as if "what people liked best were the places they stay away from." Plazas that give people the separation they say they prefer go empty. No socializing occurs there at all, not even the covert kind.

"When outdoor areas are of poor quality," Gehl says, "only strictly necessary activities occur." What you want to encourage are *optional* activities, like strolling, playing chess, eating, people-watching. "Social activities occur spontaneously, as a direct result of people moving about and being in the same place." If you accommodate covert socializing, the least demanding kind of interaction, you create the necessary conditions for overt socializing.

Benches are usually big enough for two strangers to share without feeling like they're invading each other's

personal space. In a crowded area, it's good Bench Etiquette to sit all the way to one side of an empty bench
so someone else can take the other. Maybe, after a few
minutes, you strike up a conversation with that someone. Maybe you tell them your incredible life story, how
you were a college football champion, then a war hero,
then a Ping-Pong diplomat, then a shrimping magnate
who once, for no particular reason, decided to go on a run
that lasted three years. Or maybe you don't interact at all.
Gehl admits that contacts in public spaces are "usually
very fleeting." But some simple exchanges *do* develop into
deeper ones. It's a numbers game: where more people self-
congest, more people have fleeting contacts; where more
people have fleeting contact, more acquaintances form;
where more people know one another, a friendliness in
the community grows; and that, in turn, emboldens people
to engage more with strangers.

I love Barcelona because it feels like a small town, and
that's been even more true during COVID. Here I run into
someone I know more often than in other cities I've lived
in, and it usually happens in one of the more popular public spaces. Sometimes they're with people I haven't met,
we all chat for a while, and a small city gets smaller. This
is how attractive public places can turn covert into overt
socializing. "Social events can develop spontaneously," as
Gehl says. "Visits and gatherings can be arranged on short
notice, when the mood dictates." This spontaneity is typical
of European socializing, with its centuries-old plaza culture. (Barcelona locals give me a strange look when I try to
make plans a week in advance.)

The vibrant "life between buildings" in Europe is a result of iteration as much as good design. As Gehl points out, urban planning didn't come into its own until the Renaissance, and many European city centers formed prior to that. They "evolved through a process that often took many hundreds of years . . . this slow process permitted continual adjustment and adaptation of the physical environment to the city functions. The city was not a goal in itself, but a tool formed by use." That's one reason why old towns in Europe are so pleasant to stroll through (when they're not slammed by tourists). They were honed to suit the needs of a pedestrianized public that used outdoor space as a communal living room. It's why they're often better for socializing than the planned cities that came after, the cities designed for aesthetics, for buildings, for interiors, for commuters. But demand for more and better public spaces is growing, reshaping cities across the world.

The biggest challenge? Cars.

"Pushing back the tide of cars that swamped the world's cities in the latter half of the 20th century is the next great task facing the world's urban planners," writes *Vox*'s David Roberts, "and they are beginning to take it on."

In 2019, a few months before the pandemic, Roberts published a stellar five-part series about Barcelona's ambitious plan to take back the city from cars. Like many European cities, Barcelona has an old town (Ciutat Vella) that's partly closed to automotive traffic, and there are other neighborhoods here, like Gràcia, that favor pedestrians over vehicles. But the city's large central district, Eixample,

is built on a grid pattern with wide avenues that is continuously crisscrossed by cars.

Eixample was conceived by the Catalan urban planner Il-
defons Cerdà, who invented the study of "urbanisation" in the
mid-nineteenth century. Cerdà designed the iconic, airy, oc-
tagonal blocks of Eixample—called *manzanas*—as a response
to the old town's cramped streets and housing, which were
causing severe public health issues. The wide avenues, open
interiors of the blocks, height restrictions on buildings—these
ensured that those living in Eixample would enjoy maximum
light and fresh air. In carefully considering how urban spaces
affect the well-being of residents and the community, Cerdà
was ahead of his time. His original plan called for only two
or three sides of each block to be built up. The open sides
would give on to public gardens, where locals could gather,
play games, socialize—the kind of space today's planners are
trying to carve out of concrete jungles the world over.

Barcelona could've had dozens of urban oases across
Eixample, but market forces proved too strong. Developers
built on the blocks' open sides, and the government lacked
the power to stop them. The manzanas were enclosed, and
the interiors became parking lots and private terraces. I live in
Eixample now, and my back window looks over one of these
interiors, carved into fifteen or twenty private spaces, with
an unused and inaccessible area in the center. It's a bummer
when you think of what it could have been: a public space
for the people who live in this manzana to share and enjoy,
which we could design, decorate, and maintain together. As
it is, I barely know anyone in the block.

(In the first months of COVID, when we cheered health workers from our windows each night, I saw a glimpse of what a manzana community could be—but once that ritual ended, we retreated into our flats and became strangers again.)

Now Barcelona is attempting to fix past mistakes. As Roberts details, the city has embarked on a "superblock" program, which, if successful, will transform the Catalan capital: "The basic idea of a superblock is to delineate a large area of roughly three-by-three blocks as shared use space, with bicyclists, pedestrians, and people who simply want to sit at picnic tables in the street given equal priority to cars." Vehicles will be rerouted around the superblocks, or required to drive through at extremely slow speeds. The pavement will be raised to the height of the sidewalk, letting pedestrians know they're welcome on the road, that cars must yield to them and not the other way around. On streets where cars used to speed by, parklets will appear. Children will play in the center of once-busy intersections. And there will be benches, benches galore!

At the time of this writing, Barcelona has only installed six superblocks, but the plan is to install *five hundred*, which is wild. Though the rollouts of the first few were a bit rocky, the superblocks have been welcomed by many of the people who live within them, especially when they're asked to collaborate on design.

Which is crucial. We need government to prize public spaces from the grip of market forces, but residents should ultimately be the ones who have power over urban commons, not markets *or* the state. In the hands of locals, public space can actually live up to its radical potential. As *The Guardian*'s Justin McGuirk points out, there's more to the urban commons than parks and community gardens. Public spaces can also be sites of protest and political organizing, hubs for local self-governance. The bench can be more than a place to relax. It can be seating for a neighborhood meeting, a space to plan and debate, a platform from which to address the community.

But "commons can easily become enclaves," writes McGuirk, especially when urban renewal projects trigger gentrification. This is a major challenge for the Barcelona superblocks and cities across the world: when an urban environment becomes more livable, it becomes more desirable and costs rise; when costs rise, lower-income residents get priced out. The market indirectly asserts itself on space that aimed to exclude it—with the help of people who are only willing to sacrifice so much. Too often, the beneficiaries of the commons' experiments in education, culture, transportation, etc., are the already dominant social groups—white, educated, middle- to upper-class people, like me.

Roberts points out that the most effective solution to this issue is social housing, "set aside or rent-controlled for working- or middle-class residents." The superblock planners understand and advocate this, but as with the fight against cars, social housing is easier advocated than done. It's always contentious, always an uphill battle. But it's not impossible to achieve. Cities like Vienna have managed to dramatically expand affordable housing, which gives diverse groups access to all the city has to offer, including a say and a stake in the urban commons. There's no reason that other cities can't accomplish the same.

The public bench should be a symbol of inclusion. Unfortunately, it's recently become a symbol of the opposite. In an effort to remove homeless people from public spaces, several cities have been reducing public seating and retrofitting what remains with "hostile architecture," design features that aim to curb behaviors the local government deems unwanted. If you live in any major American city, you've no doubt seen this stuff: benches with metal armrests bolted between individual seats, to prevent someone from lying down; spikes or bumps that line the tops of ledges and other flat surfaces. New York City recently introduced "leaning bars" in some subway stations, angled pieces of wood that disallow sitting.

Paired with loitering laws and sit-lie ordinances, hostile architecture aims to make public space unusable for those who need it most. It cruelly harms the homeless, without addressing the root causes of their predicament, and it makes the city feel unwelcome to all. Its effect, in other words, is the opposite of its foul intention.

As Whyte says, "Places designed with distrust get what they were looking for."

If there is anything that the COVID pandemic proved, it's that every city dweller needs access to good-quality public space, and the aim of that space should be to invite, not restrict. Because of limitations on indoor gatherings, cities got a unique chance to experiment. Streets were blocked off to make room for improvised restaurant terraces or to allow more social distancing space for strollers. Like sitting on a bench, *flânerie* was pretty much the only available activity for months. It's always a little exciting when you can walk on a street meant for cars, when you transgress the conventional uses of a city's architecture. Urban planning trains you to see the environment in one way, concealing alternative perspectives. But as soon as you break the rules, a new city snaps into focus, a new relationship with the environment becomes possible, obvious. Once people get a taste of something they like, something better, it becomes very difficult to take it away from them. That's why COVID has thrown accelerant on urban renewal projects around the world.

I saw Barcelona change overnight.

Last May, I woke to an odd sight below my window: one of the two lanes on the street in front of my building was painted with thick yellow lines. On the edge of that lane was a series of long concrete slabs, spaced about fifteen feet apart. I thought maybe it was for a construction project, which is always happening somewhere in the city. Later, I noticed a man walking on the yellow lane, then a couple sitting on a concrete slab. I went downstairs to investigate: the lane reached in both directions as far as I could see. So did the slabs. A couple days later, I read that Barcelona was widening sidewalks to comply with social distancing requirements. By then everyone had already figured it out. As the city came out of lockdown, people took to the new pedestrian corridor with enthusiasm, as if it had always been there. The slabs, of course, were public benches. Why they chose that design, I don't know. They're not pretty or especially comfortable, but people don't seem to care about that—and they're not hostile.

It's May again. Over the last year I've watched my street come to life. I've seen Whyte's obvious maxim borne out in real time: "People tend to sit most where there are places to sit." Walk a few blocks down Carrer del Consell de Cent and you'll see it, too: friends chatting and couples kissing, people reading or eating or texting (or reading texts while eating), homeless people, elderly people, tourists, coworkers, and students—lots of students.

Opposite my apartment, there's a vocational school. Each morning, at about eleven a.m., students spill out onto the street and crowd the benches on my block. I hear them now, in fact, from the open window in my office. They're laughing in that accusatory way that suggests someone has done or said something stupid. I head over to the window. Some of the students are sitting on the benches. Others are sitting cross-legged on the yellow lane itself, their bookbags scattered everywhere, as if this were their own living room. I guess it is. It's everyone's.

In November 2020, Barcelona mayor Ada Colau announced that the new pedestrian corridors would become permanent—and that was just the beginning. Not only will the existing makeshift lanes be revamped, but a ten-year, $46 million plan aims to transform *one in three* Eixample streets into a "green zone." This, in effect, makes the entire barrio of Eixample one giant superblock. With a few exceptions, vehicle traffic will be allowed only around the neighborhood's perimeter, while twenty-one intersections will become new pedestrian plazas and twenty-one streets will become "green axes," planted with trees. In total, there will be 16 new acres of green space and 82.5

new acres of pedestrian space. No one in Eixample will live more than two hundred meters from public green space. Cerdà would be overjoyed.

Just think of the benches! The perspectives! Think of all the people to watch, the time to waste, the Modernist masterpieces to admire. Think of the sunlight cutting across their facades, the sunlight on your skin, the heat in the iron armrests. Think of the bonds made between parents as their kids play in new plazas. Think of the protests and the community gardens, the overt and covert socializing, the friends and the strangers. Think of all that mean egotism vanishing on planter ledges and stairs, concrete slabs and chairs. Think of sitting back, breathing in the scene, and dissolving . . .

THINKING IN OEUVRES

Chapter One: Umbilical Cord

"You're saying you got *ten* movies in you?" Film critic Peter Travers was scandalized, his pitch climbing with every word. He gestured with panicky hands and repeated the question, to be sure: "And this is it, after ten?"

Tarantino tried to respond: "That's kind of—"

"WHAT ARE YOU TALKING ABOUT, QUENTIN!?"

Find the clip to see for yourself: the man is befuddled. And he's not the only one:

The Hollywood Reporter's Stephen Galloway shares the feeling: "Are you seriously only going to do ten?"

So does Harry Smith from NBC's *Today*: "Are you really only going to make one more movie?"

And Jimmy Kimmel: "Is this really going to be your second-to-last movie? You're really going to do one more and that's it?"

Virginia Trioli, cohost of Australia's *News Breakfast*

morning show, gave Mr. Tarantino a chance to take it back: "Do you regret vowing that you'd only make ten films? Are you sticking with that promise?"

Russian reporter Eugene Rybov just wanted to make sure he was understanding correctly: "Once upon a time you said you shoot only ten movies. Here in Russia we all hope that this is just a bad joke, just some kind of lost in translation."

Travers and the rest can't accept that someone like Tarantino would impose retirement *on himself*, while he's still relatively young, still in fighting shape, while he has the kind of creative freedom few filmmakers ever enjoy. It goes against a basic Rule of Success in Hollywood: once you've arrived at the party, hang around until someone tells you to leave. Unaccustomed to people who flout this rule, they assume he's bluffing or misguided, maybe both. After all, how many people fight their entire careers for an invite to the party and never get one? How many enter, then immediately get shown the door? Few leave by choice; fewer still are begged to stay. That's essentially what these reporters are doing: begging Tarantino to carry on, to entertain us for a little while longer.

Don't abandon us to a future of infinite shared multiverse reboot sequels, Quentin, not yet!

Must be one hell of an ego boost.

While I'm sure Tarantino loves to hear talk show hosts plead for more, he has better reasons for early retirement. "I like the idea of being defined by a filmography," he told Rybov, "that was all artistic and by intention, as opposed to just working because I don't know how to stop."

"I think a lot of directors," he explained to Kimmel, "they talk about, 'Oh, I wanna do this thing and that thing, I have time to do this and time to do that.' But I actually think they have far less time than they think they do. . . . If I think I only have two movies, well, that keeps it at the tip of the spear, if you know what I mean. That means those ones better be good."

"I like the idea," he soothed Travers, "that there is an umbilical cord connected to my first film all the way to my last, and then that is the body of work, 'cause I am about my filmography. And frankly, I do feel bad films on the filmography affect good films on the filmography."

Quentin Tarantino thinks in *oeuvres*, the fancy and hard-to-pronounce French word for "body of work." That in itself doesn't make him unique. Most artists consider the arc of their life's work, especially when that life nears its end. They might look back and discover some big themes in their career. They might try to divide it into chapters or phases, or even agree to a retrospective. It's natural to think about legacy, and the most lasting legacies usually come from oeuvres, not single works: Shakespeare, Picasso, the Beatles, Beyoncé, Dickens, Hitchcock, Morrison, Miyazaki. Tarantino would love to join this list, as many other artists would. Like many other artists, he'll submit his oeuvre to posterity for consideration. What makes Tarantino unusual is that, while most artists look *back* at their body of work, he's been carefully shaping his own from the start. For him, the filmography itself is a work of art.

Just as great movies shouldn't have weak scenes, great filmographies shouldn't have weak movies. Like bad performances can spoil a good script, lesser projects can spoil a legacy. That's what Tarantino believes. He's eager to avoid the major/minor game that film nerds like me play with revered filmmakers. *Shutter Island* is minor Scorsese, we might say, compared to major works like *Raging Bull* and *Taxi Driver*. *Girl 6* is minor Spike Lee, next to *Malcolm X* and *Do the Right Thing*. These "minor" movies often appear toward the end of a career. Alfred Hitchcock's final five films barely register against his many masterpieces. Lopping them off the filmography wouldn't diminish his reputation. In fact, Tarantino might argue that Hitchcock's legacy would be *even greater* today if he'd walked away from cinema in 1963 and not 1976.

Artists don't always notice when their skills are flagging, so Tarantino is quitting early to prevent crossing that line unwittingly. Ten movies are enough for a good, healthy filmography—it's three less than Kubrick, but three more than Tarkovsky—and the nine he's made so far are all pretty good. He began with the electric *Reservoir Dogs*, followed it up with *Pulp Fiction*, an era-defining masterpiece, and his most recent movie, *Once Upon a Time in Hollywood*, ranks among his best. Not every release in between reaches these peaks (*Death Proof* and *The Hateful Eight* are my least favorite), but I don't think Tarantino's made any real clunkers. That's my opinion, of course. You're welcome to disagree, something film nerds love to do.

You might not be a fan of Tarantino's style or my opinion of it. But for the purposes of this essay, you don't have to be. I'm less interested in the quality of his movies than in his perspective on oeuvre, what he or any artist might

gain by thinking of their career holistically. It's clear Tarantino sees a reputational value in having a body of work that
maintains a high standard, that's free of dead weight. But is
there a value to the work itself? Can a well-designed oeuvre bestow greater meaning onto the projects that make it
up? Can a body of work be a work of art?

Chapter Two: Heart to Heart

To answer these questions, I searched for other artists who
shared Quentin Tarantino's obsession with oeuvre.

I found William Butler Yeats.

An Irish poet working in the late nineteenth and early
twentieth centuries, Yeats wrote some of the most powerful verse of his or any time. As a Symbolist, he believed
reality could be described only *indirectly*, with the aid of
metaphor and allusion. So he mined the images of myth,
mysticism, and magic and channeled their symbolic power
to cast light on human nature. He was a master of rhythm
and form; to read him is to be entranced. Unlike Hitchcock, he improved to the very end. Like Tarantino, he em-
braced a macro perspective on his art.

"His project, always, was to give his work organic unity,"
writes John Unterecker in *A Reader's Guide to William Butler Yeats*. "Everything, he felt, should fit into a whole . . .
Yeats reworked many of his poems and plays, rearranging
the sequence of the poems so that they would construct
harmonious units, dropping any of those that did not fit
into the grand scheme."

Yeats went further than Tarantino has. He revised and even removed previous work to strengthen his oeuvre. Yeats viewed his body of work as a living thing, always open to change if he found a better image or turn of phrase, or if his thinking changed and suddenly his new poetry fell out of sync with his old. That was permission enough to modify a stanza or two for better consistency. "One day when I was twenty-three or twenty-four," he recalled in 1919, "this sentence seemed to form in my head, without my willing it, much as sentences form when we are half-asleep: 'Hammer your thoughts into unity.'"

Did he achieve that unity? If so, how? And if so, what did he accomplish by doing it? Absolute unity is probably an impossible ambition, Unterecker argues, but Yeats came as close as any artist to realizing it, and he did this by organizing his work around recurring people, images, and systems. Take a look at his most famous poem, for example, "The Second Coming":

> *Turning and turning in the widening gyre*
> *The falcon cannot hear the falconer;*
> *Things fall apart; the center cannot hold;*
> *Mere anarchy is loosed upon the world,*
> *The blood-dimmed tide is loosed, and everywhere*
> *The ceremony of innocence is drowned;*
> *The best lack all conviction, while the worst*
> *Are full of passionate intensity.*
>
> *Surely some revelation is at hand;*
> *Surely the Second Coming is at hand.*

The Second Coming! Hardly are those words out
When a vast image out of Spiritus Mundi
Troubles my sight: somewhere in the sands of
　　the desert
A shape with lion body and the head of a man,
A gaze blank and pitiless as the sun,
Is moving its slow thighs, while all about it
Reel shadows of the indignant desert birds.
The darkness drops again; but now I know
That twenty centuries of stony sleep
Were vexed to nightmare by a rocking cradle,
And what rough beast, its hour come round at last,
Slouches toward Bethlehem to be born?

You don't have to know Yeats's ideology to get something from this poem. "The Second Coming" describes a nightmarish vision at the end of an era when the norms that organized it come undone, and bad actors rule in "the blood-dimmed tide" of anarchy that ensues. A new age dawns, but the Second Coming has a sinister feel, "a gaze blank and pitiless as the sun." This revelation takes the form of a "rough beast." It may deliver us from the present dysfunction . . . but into what?

The story itself is remarkably potent. It has the uncanny quality nightmares have of being general yet personal, and the more you think about it, the more the story seems to find real-world analogues: Could the rough beast, a terror that inaugurates a new world, could it be a war? A revolution? What about a global pandemic? Can't you see the "worst full of passionate intensity" in the lead-up to the Great Recession, the housing bubble slouching toward Wall Street to burst? The prophecy of the poem can fit a range of historical events, even ones that haven't yet reached their climax, like climate change.

Yeats wrote the poem in the wake of World War I, a conflict that saw death and destruction on an unprecedented scale. Four years of that—plus the Russian Revolution, a flu pandemic, and the start of the Irish War of Independence—left Europe in a cynical mood. Yeats felt it. Maybe the center *wouldn't* hold. Maybe things *would* fall apart. Maybe they already had. It wasn't absurd to see that moment as a kind of apocalypse. The poem reflects that view. And as much as every generation thinks its crisis is *the* hinge point of history, "The Second Coming" will continue to find resonances.

But there's something more systematic at work here.

Around this time, Yeats created a philosophy of history that reflected his many interests, and "The Second Coming" is also an expression of that. The system is far too elaborate to explain in detail, but the basic idea is this:

History develops in two-thousand-year cycles, represented by Yeats as interpenetrating cones called *gyres*. Every new era is born from the ashes of the old. It grows, reaches its peak, wanes, and eventually collapses into the next era, which will have opposite values to the one preceding it. Yeats believed that the birth of Christ was the start of the current cycle, and his system predicts the Christian era will end by AD 2100. The title of "The Second Coming" recalls the biblical idea of Revelation, but the era to come will bear little resemblance to the Christian era, and as the poem makes clear, its messiah will be radically different from Jesus Christ.

Once you know Yeats's ideology, it's impossible to see "The Second Coming" as a stand-alone piece. Like all his poems, it's a thread in a larger tapestry, and the questions it poses have responses elsewhere in the oeuvre. In "Two Songs from a Play," for example, published almost a decade after "The Second Coming," Yeats looks at the implications of his theory by turning back the clock two thousand years to the ending of the previous historical cycle:

> *I saw a staring virgin stand*
> *Where holy Dionysus died,*
> *And tear the heart out of his side.*
> *And lay the heart upon her hand*
> *And bear that beating heart away;*
> *And then did all the Muses sing*
> *Of Magnus Annus at the spring,*
> *As though God's death were but a play.*

The first stanza mixes figures from two religious traditions. The "staring virgin" is the Virgin Mary, and "holy Dionysus" is a Greek god of wine, fertility, and festivity. In the Greek myth, Athena retrieves Dionysus's heart after he's dismembered by the Titans, and gives it to Zeus, who resurrects him. In Yeats's version, Mary takes the heart instead, to bear a new god and a new epoch. The Classical Age gives way to the Christian Age, just as the Christian Age gives way to the rough beast in "The Second Coming." Yeats goes on:

Another Troy must rise and set,
Another lineage feed the crow,
Another Argo's painted prow
Drive to a flashier bauble yet.
The Roman Empire stood appalled:
It dropped the reins of peace and war
When that fierce virgin and her Star
Out of the fabulous darkness called.

Things repeat in cycles, Yeats says: the gyre will widen again, Troy will again let that huge wooden horse inside its walls. What's disturbing is the weary tone—*another, another, another*—repetitive like the historical cycles, but repetition without progress or a sense of renewal.

Then he switches perspectives to the people on the ground. The coming of Jesus shocks and horrifies the Roman world, which has ruled for so long. Mary and "her Star" arrive from the "fabulous darkness" and change everything. Is this how *we* might react to the arrival of the rough beast? Is this how historical change is always experienced? To an old guard, change can seem to materialize out of darkness, enigmatic and appalling.

In pity for man's darkening thought
He walked that room and issued thence
In Galilean turbulence;
The Babylonian starlight brought
A fabulous, formless darkness in;
Odour of blood when Christ was slain

Made all Platonic tolerance vain
And vain all Doric discipline.

Not only does Christ arrive out of darkness, as we saw in the previous stanza, but he brings a "fabulous, formless darkness" with him—he *is* that darkness. Yeats paraphrases the Neo-Platonist philosopher Antoninus, who watched the rising tide of Christianity in the fourth century and worried that "a fabulous and formless darkness is about to tyrannize over all that is beautiful on Earth." Beautiful things like the "Platonic tolerance" of multicultural, polytheistic Rome. Does something equally brilliant replace these beauties? No. It's something repulsive: the overwhelming odor of Christ's blood.

Everything that man esteems
Endures a moment or a day.
Love's pleasure drives his love away,
The painter's brush consumes his dreams;
The herald's cry, the soldier's tread
Exhaust his glory and his might:
Whatever flames upon the night
Man's own resinous heart has fed.

In the astonishing final stanza of "Two Songs from a Play," the grand cycles of history disappear. Yeats's convoluted system of gyres yields to a lucid observation about life: *all things must pass.* Life follows the same pattern as history, as Jesus and Dionysus: birth, death, and resurrection.

But resurrection, as Yeats makes clear in the earlier stanzas, doesn't guarantee progress. What's guaranteed is that rebirths will be rocky, marked by darkness and ruin—or at least that's how they'll feel to those who live through them. Transience and turbulence are the only sure things. All we can do is endure, captive to the tides and the rough beasts of our time. History slouches over us all, while the muses sing.

Depressing, right?

Yeats had a morbid fascination with decay and death. "When I was a boy everybody talked about progress," he once wrote, "and rebellion against my elders took the form of aversion to that myth . . . I felt a sort of ecstasy at the contemplation of ruin." There was plenty of ruin to contemplate in his lifetime—much of it senseless. It was hard not to feel caught in the currents of history, easy to feel powerless. To recapture some agency, Yeats fit current events into a grand system. But that only raised the issue of agency again. If you could really find the pattern of history, what space does that leave for human beings to influence it? He confronts this question in the final two lines of the poem, which arrive like a sudden reversal:

> *Whatever flames upon the night*
> *Man's own resinous heart has fed.*

It's true that the currents of history govern human thought, that we dream what our time permits us to dream, but it's also true that those currents are *created* by human thought. It's a feedback loop: history makes us and we make history. The bulk of the poem emphasizes the tragedy of the former, but the ending offers a counterpoint in this dazzling circular image: man's "resinous heart" *feeding* all that "flames upon the night," ultimately *consumed* by that same fire. For this reason, critic David A. Ross argues, "the poem ends with a flourish of defiant humanism," with an appeal to creativity in the face of ruin and giant historical forces. This ending does not negate the poem's weary, pessimistic tone, but it does qualify it.

This is what all Yeats's poems do: they expand, deepen, and qualify the other poems in the oeuvre. "Two Songs from a Play" adds definition to the nightmare vision of "The Second Coming." It helps us to understand Yeats's anxieties about the transformations in his world. It places the rough beast in a line with Jesus and Dionysus, explores the cyclical nature of human affairs, shows us that perspectives can change dramatically in the fullness of time. It tempers the fatalism of "The Second Coming" with a note of defiance, even hope. In the first poem, we are defenseless against that vast image out of Spiritus Mundi. In the last lines of "Two Songs from a Play," Yeats restores some power to the creative, if flammable, human heart.

And it doesn't end there. You can track these themes up and down his body of work. You can take any image out of either of those poems—blood, gyre, birds, fire—and trace their usages across the oeuvre. Every usage modifies every other, layering meaning on meaning, until images evolve into symbols that support immense complexity. This is all intentional. No word in a Yeats poem was ever chosen carelessly. No line ever constructed without consideration of the greater architecture.

Take the word "heart," for example.

As we've just seen, Yeats places the heart at the center of a great historical process. Its desires are the engine of cultural change and also the fuel. And yet, despite its major role in the drama of history, the human heart is "resinous," like the gooey, flammable stuff that oozes from tree trunks. The heart is our link to the perishable world, an image of mortality. For Yeats, this makes it the perfect symbol to contrast with the eternal realm of beauty and art, which preoccupied his mind in later life. In "Sailing to Byzantium," published in the same book as "Two Songs from a Play," he implores the sages of "the holy city of Byzantium" to

> *Consume my heart away; sick with desire,*
> *And fastened to a dying animal*
> *It knows not what it is; and gather me*
> *Into the artifice of eternity.* *

Another image of a heart devoured. Yeats longs to escape the prison of the body, which decays in old age like a "dying animal." He longs to escape his heart, sick with desires that make it combustible, and fuse with eternity. Here, heart aligns with sick and dying animals, and opposes what is immortal and outside of nature. But Yeats longs in vain. As he complains in the next poem, called "The Tower," he is trapped within his body:

---

* All **bolding** is my own.

What shall I do with this absurdity—
O heart, O troubled heart—*this caricature,*
Decrepit age that has been tied to me,
As to a dog's tail?

Unable to escape from his decaying heart, Yeats looks elsewhere for consolation. In "Meditations in Time of Civil War," he reflects on a gift he received from Junzo Sato: a five-hundred-year-old ancestral sword. Taken by its beauty, he memorializes the antique weapon in verse:

Chaucer had not drawn breath
When it was forged. In Sato's house,
Curved like new moon, moon-luminous
It lay five hundred years.
Yet if no change appears
No moon; **only an aching heart**
Conceives a changeless work of art.

Looking on Sato's sword, Yeats comes to a realization. Though he can't escape his body and join with eternity, he can *create* something that will, "a changeless work of art." What's more, it's only a human heart, an aching heart sick with desire, that could produce such a timeless creation. Maybe there's some solace in that thought.

Or maybe that's too simple. After all, Sato's sword isn't *really* changeless, is it? It's survived for half a millennium, but it won't last forever. A student of the destructive nature of history, Yeats can't blind himself to the basic impermanence of things, even the best works of art. So what solace is there? Is there any comfort against age, death, the fading away of our work? Yeats takes up the question in "Vacillation." He offers some potential answers, but, predictably, vacillates. Eventually he recognizes that impermanence itself might be the only truth that matters:

> *From man's **blood-sodden heart** are sprung*
> *Those branches of night and day*
> *Where the gaudy moon is hung.*
> *What's the meaning of all song?*
> *'Let all things pass away.'*

Five years later, Yeats returns to the concluding lesson of "Two Songs from a Play," again choosing the heart as his symbol. The subject is the same, but the imagery is different. The "resinous" heart is now "blood-sodden" and planted in fertile ground to grow a tree. As in "Meditations in Time of Civil War," the heart is the source of our creations, but such creations are not changeless or out of nature. Like us, they are transitory, vacillating, emphatically *in nature.* Coming to terms with that doesn't have to be depressing. In "Vacillation," Yeats finds tranquility in the thought, even joy. He understands that transience is the highest theme for the artist, while eternity is only a mirage.

Empowered by that awareness, Yeats rode this "tragic joy" to the end of his life. In 1939, the year of his death at seventy-three, his final volume was published, called *Last Poems.* In "The Circus Animals' Desertion," Yeats trawls back through his poetry and revisits the characters and images he worked with for so long. He dwells on "themes of the embittered heart" and "heart mysteries." He wonders if he loved his poetic myths too much, instead of "those things that they were emblems of." At the end of his career and life, he finally reflects on where those images came from. In very nearly his final lines, he adds one last meaning to a fruitful symbol:

> . . . *Now that my ladder's gone*
> *I must lie down where all the ladders start*
> **In the foul rag and bone shop of the heart.**

In the nineteenth century, rag-and-bone men scavenged unwanted household items and sold them to merchants. That's what Yeats envisions as the poet's job: to scavenge items from the heart and sell them to the public, to weave all that detritus into images and stories and truth. The heart is the well into which any artist must descend for raw materials. It is the seed of the tree of man's transience. It's the locus of great historical cycles, what Mary tears from Dionysus's side to birth the Christian Age. It's the "troubled" heart, the "trembling" heart, the "burning," "wild," "importunate" heart. It's the heart that "could bear no more," that "drifts through the violet air," the heart that "laughter made sweet," that "troubles your peace." "I cast my heart into my rhymes," he tells us, and we see that he did, again and again and again.

By the time of his death, "heart" vibrates with meanings. It becomes a spring-loaded word, ready to explode across any line or verse, expanding, deepening. Yeats built his symbols meticulously, line by line, until he created an arsenal versatile enough for any subject. And if you're familiar with his poetry and come across one of his favorite symbols, you can't help but recall the other poems in which it was used, how it was used, and what you felt about it. His oeuvre resembles one of those detective pinboards you see on TV, where the case is arrayed over a large surface—news clippings, photographs, evidence—all of it linked by crisscrossing red twine. Touch one piece, set the twine quivering, and your eyes start dashing back and forth. It's silly to think of Yeats's poems as individual units when each one contains insights from every other.

Can a body of work be a work of art? Yes. Yeats proves that beyond a doubt, I think. While each poem has a completeness of its own, the overall unity is his ultimate expression. Its wisdom is dense and complex. The "answers" it offers are not easy or even consistent. They're often contradictory, but that's not a weakness of the oeuvre. Yeats never aimed for a logician's unity. His body of work doesn't resemble a proof, so much as it does a human personality, which we know is full of ambiguity and contradiction. Yeats's work vacillates like a person does, like he did. It probes stubborn questions about existence from every angle. It draws on the oeuvres of other great thinkers, tests its insights against the insights of genius. It's confident and timid, exuberant and grave, epic and intimate. It gives off sparks, even now. Even now, it lives.

Chapter Three: The Goods

What about Tarantino? Snobs might balk at comparing the Nobel laureate Yeats with a filmmaker who once staged a fight in which fifty-plus people are killed/dismembered by a samurai sword–wielding woman in a yellow jumpsuit— but what do they know?

The more I researched Yeats and Tarantino, the more they seemed to me kindred artists. I'm not sure either of them would agree with that, Yeats in particular—though I like to imagine he would've had fun at *Kill Bill*. A few similarities jump out: They're both perfectionists. They're both expert craftsmen with deep and broad (in the case of Tarantino, encyclopedic) knowledge of their media. Their works overflow with references to past masters. They are both respected among peers, both dwell on legacy, both think in oeuvres. Most of all, they're both *obsessive*.

Yeats was obsessed with mysticism and the occult. He pored over dense and obscure texts, extracting whatever patterns he found there, and used them to give his work structure. The uniqueness of his style stems in part from his reliance on sources that "serious" artists wouldn't even look at, let alone read or use.

Tarantino is obsessed with cinema, specifically genre cinema and the various subgenres they fracture into. He has a particular love for exploitation film, low-budget B movies that "exploit" an audience's desire for violence, sex, and other cheap thrills. Like mysticism, pulpy genre movies comprise a dense and obscure text, one that "serious" filmmakers and film critics long ignored and disparaged.

Tarantino, delighted by lowbrow cinema from a young age, extracted the patterns he found there and used them to give his work structure. On their own, his films are sophisticated in the ways they manipulate and combine generic tropes, without forgetting to honor their payoffs (to "deliver the goods," as Tarantino likes to say). Together, they make a case for the worth of critically neglected filmmaking, and for the larger significance of genre itself.

The two artists' aims are different, of course. Yeats wanted to answer humanity's deepest questions, to unravel the meaning of life and the pattern of history—you know, small stuff. Poetry was the means to these ends. For Tarantino, film is a means *and* an end. He uses cinema to say something about cinema, about what it can do. This is why his work is sometimes criticized as a "callow triumph of technique over substance." But that view is as shallow as it claims Tarantino is—partly because there's a great deal of substance in his films, partly because genre is a rich subject matter, more than worthy of an artist's focus. What unites these two isn't the scope of their oeuvres, but their awareness of its value as a creative tool.

After Tarantino released *Reservoir Dogs* in 1992, critic Gavin Smith predicted the movie would "prove pivotal in the history of American independent film, for legitimizing its relationship to Hollywood genre." Smith implies a conflict between genre and independent film, and in some ways there is. Hollywood uses genre to serve its commercial interests. Its predictable structures are perfect for mass-market storytelling. This is why film genre is often associated with superficiality, cynicism, and the profit motive. Independent film, on the other hand, is associated with art cinema. Lower budgets mean less pressure to appeal to a wide audience, means more freedom to engage difficult and controversial subjects. Independent films don't have to use genre's formulas. They don't have to end with a kiss, or with the villain captured, or with the last stupid teenager escaping from the haunted house.

But these are simplistic categories. Hollywood genre films can be artistic and independent films can be commercial.* Independent film is also a *source* of genre film. Horror, for example, is a film genre that can be produced for cheap, yet few independent horror movies would be considered art cinema (despite the recent wave of art-horror.) "Independent," "studio," "genre," and "art" are labels that can be mixed and matched in different ways.

So when Smith says *Reservoir Dogs* legitimizes the relationship between independent film and Hollywood genre, is he right? Did it need legitimizing? By the early nineties, there had already been lots of independent genre work, movies like *Mean Streets* (1973, crime film), *Annie Hall* (1977, romantic comedy), and *Blood Simple* (1984, film noir). Many of these "revisionist" films helped to establish genre as a locus of high art, and they all came out before *Reservoir Dogs*. What makes Tarantino's genre obsession different?

In Tarantino's aesthetics, writes Eyal Peretz, "nothing is ever simply or really itself; every single gesture seems always to be marked by its own cinematic nature, as belonging to a

---

* In fact, a lot of "indie" studios are actually owned by the majors—Focus Features (owned by Comcast), Searchlight Pictures (owned by Disney), Sony Picture Classics (owned by Sony).

genre, or being a quotation or the performance of a role." In other words, *Tarantino forces us to see genre*. In other genre movies, story may be bound by certain rules, but "the on-screen content is presented as 'natural,' not as something framed by the genre and its conventions."

Even a film as genre-based as Spielberg's *Raiders of the Lost Ark* (1981)—an adventure movie that intentionally modernizes early-twentieth-century serials like *Buck Rogers* and *Zorro's Fighting Legion*—attempts to blur the edges of the frame. It winks at its antecedents, but that's all. The movie does not want to call attention to its movie-ness. For Spielberg, that would defeat the point. It would break the "suspension of disbelief."

For Tarantino, the point is already defeated; according to him, suspension of disbelief isn't worth aiming for because it doesn't really exist. "That's a theory that I don't think is actually a practice," he told Stephen Colbert in 2015. "I always know I'm watching a movie." Whether or not he's right, Tarantino makes sure *we* always know his movies are movies when we're watching them. *Reservoir Dogs* isn't just a film about a heist. It's a heist film about a heist, and from the very beginning that crime film subgenre is made visible to the viewer:

After the long chat about Madonna and tipping etiquette that opens the movie, the "dogs" exit the diner in matching black suits, while "Little Green Bag" by George Baker Selection plays, under credits. Here the film quotes a classic of the heist subgenre, 1960's *Ocean's 11*, which ends with exactly the same imagery: suited robbers walking together, looking cool, under credits. Jean-Pierre Melville's

1966 heist film, *Le Deuxième Souffle*, features the image again: robbers clad in black suits, fedoras, and trench coats walking along a mountain road. The suits appear yet again in John Woo's *A Better Tomorrow II* (1987), a crime/action classic of Hong Kong cinema. We've barely made it eight minutes before a raft of quotes leads us back through the history of the heist movie, situating *Reservoir Dogs* firmly within its generic legacy.

This is what Peretz means when he says "every single gesture seems always to be marked by its own cinematic nature." Tarantino wants us to see the marks of genre in every frame. And we do, even if we don't (and couldn't possibly) share his exhaustive knowledge of cinema, even if we don't catch all the quotes. As media consumers, we're educated enough to pick up on the markers of specific genres, whether or not we can place their sources. You might not know, for example, that when Mr. White says to Mr. Blonde in that diner scene, "You shoot me in a dream, you better wake up and apologize," he's quoting James Cagney from the 1938 gangster film *Angels with Dirty Faces,* but you know it's the kind of wisecrack a gangster might make. Eventually those markers make it into the cultural drinking water. In the decades since *Reservoir Dogs* came out, our familiarity with all kinds of media has grown exponentially, but it was already good enough in '92 for Tarantino to craft a movie out of it.

For all the twists he puts on the heist film, several of the classic tropes remain intact: a group of thieves organize a jewel heist, after crime lord Joe Cabot (played by Lawrence Tierney, famous for his mobster roles in the

1940s) tips them off to a "shipment of polished stones" moving through a diamond wholesaler in Los Angeles. As the savvy filmgoer might guess, the heist goes off the rails. The criminals turn on one another before the police arrive and finish them off. These are ingredients you can find in a thousand movie capers, about which *Reservoir Dogs* is self-aware. Talk about a colorful group of thieves. The names of these thieves . . . are actually colors!

The ingredient *Reservoir Dogs* lacks is the one that's most fundamental to the genre: the heist itself. After the opening scene, the movie jumps forward to the post-heist. Through flashbacks, Tarantino fills in some of what happened before the crime, but we don't see a second of the robbery itself. All we get is the characters' stories as they scramble to figure out how it all went belly-up. This omission is *Reservoir Dogs*'s biggest spin on the genre.

Another spin is Tarantino's characterizations of the dogs, namely, the way they talk. As Tarantino says, "Gangsters don't just talk about gangster-plot-related stuff and just polish their bullets. . . . They talk about songs on the radio. They talk about the chicken dinner they had last night." This realism humanizes his genre characters and provides a comedic counterpoint to the film's convulsions of violence. Still another spin is the nonlinear narrative technique Tarantino uses (and became famous for). *Reservoir Dogs* rearranges plot points to prompt more engagement from its audience.

Tarantino spins the heist film, but doesn't revolutionize it and doesn't try to. He's not looking to transcend genre in the way many revisionist movies seek to do. He's not using genre as a tool to get somewhere else. Tarantino sees value in its formulas and tropes and payoffs. He may use our expectations against us, updating the genre for a savvy modern viewer, but he ultimately wants to reaffirm its power as a narrative form. He wants to deliver the goods.

"The art of the horror film," writes film theorist Carol Clover in *Men, Women, and Chain Saws*, which Tarantino cites as an influence, "is to a very large extent *the art of rendition or performance*, and it's understood as such by the competent audience. A particular example may have original features, but its quality as a horror film lies in the way it delivers the cliché."* You could swap horror for any genre, and the point would hold. With his wide knowledge, Tarantino *performs* genre better than any other filmmaker. He delivers the cliché with gusto.

Look at *Pulp Fiction*. Staying with the crime film, Tarantino weaves together three of the genre's most cliché scenarios:

1. Two hitmen execute a hit
2. Boxer who was supposed to throw the fight doesn't
3. Underling takes out the boss's daughter

These are stock situations from the rag-and-bone shop of the genre. And we know how they go: the hit goes wrong, the boxer has to run, the underling defies the most important rule: look but don't touch. As in *Reservoir Dogs*,

---

* Italics are my own.

Tarantino spins the stories in exciting ways. He uses the nonlinear narrative technique to great effect. He uses our familiarity with the crime film against us, to thrill and surprise. The result is a virtuosic *performance* of genre, an affirmation of its myths, created from a tapestry of its most archetypal narratives.

Like "Two Songs from a Play" does to "The Second Coming," *Pulp Fiction* deepens and expands *Reservoir Dogs*'s perspective on genre. It begins to bring Tarantino's larger project into focus.

Tarantino's third movie, *Jackie Brown*, concludes a trilogy of films in the crime genre and tightens that focus again. It's adapted from a novel by Elmore Leonard, another big influence on Tarantino. "Elmore Leonard, in his books, would always throw all these kinds of monkey wrenches that just smacked true of life," Tarantino said in 1992. "Cops are chasing after a character, character is running down a street, they commandeer a car, throw the person out, jump in the car—*but it's a stick shift and they don't drive stick!* That's real life. It kinda fucks up the genre moment. . . . That's what I'm always trying to do." Like Tarantino, Leonard fucks with genre lovingly, not to dismantle, but to reenergize it. Like Tarantino, Leonard honors the payoffs of genre fiction. He delivers the goods.

So what are these goods? Joyce Carol Oates puts it best: "However plot-ridden, fantastical, or absurd, whatever pseudo-characters, *genre fiction is always resolved.*"*

She was writing about literature, but the idea applies to any kind of fiction. Earlier, I dismissed genre endings

---

* Italics are my own.

as facile—the lover's kiss, the villain bested, the last teen-ager alive—but they are not facile by definition. Tarantino aims to prove that. *Jackie Brown* ends in the most cliché of ways: with a romantic kiss, before the hero drives into the sunset, having overcome the forces arrayed against her, a bag of cash in the trunk. Shallow as it reads, this ending is anything but. When *Jackie Brown* arrives at its resolution, after two hours of gripping, character-driven storytelling, it offers a closure that is profoundly reward-ing for the viewer. It satisfies in a way that is unique to genre fiction.

Tarantino's engagement with genre becomes extreme in his fourth movie, *Kill Bill*, an epic revenge saga divided into two volumes and several chapters.* Each chapter adopts its own genre, has its own arc and mini resolution, as The Bride kills her way to a final confrontation with the titular big bad. In its genre travelogue, *Kill Bill* visits the Samurai epic, the kung fu revenge flick, the Spaghetti Western, the Blaxploitation film, anime, and more. It's a symphony of genre, with references beyond count. If his prior films drew heavily from film history, *Kill Bill* seems to be assembled out of it, a true pastiche.

This is what Stanford professor Jean Ma calls "Taran-tino's manic referentiality, his self-conscious forging of a directorial style from an intertextual network that ex-tends downward into the trash bin of film history." What keeps the film from being derivative is its hybrid nature, Tarantino's peerless talent for mix and match. Who else

---

* *Kill Bill* is technically two movies, *Kill Bill: Volume 1* and *Kill Bill: Volume 2*, but Tarantino counts them as a single entry in his oeuvre.

could take all those fragments and fuse them into a coherent narrative? Who else would even try?

With *Kill Bill*, Tarantino advances toward the mythic. The Bride's quest for revenge plays like a classic saga, complete with trials, betrayals, and a wise mentor. She has the winds of destiny at her back. The finale feels inevitable, yet perils along the way remain thrilling. We know the movie will end how its title predicts—she will kill Bill—but that doesn't rob the story of its drama. More than other film genres (with the possible exception of horror), revenge narratives depend on the art of performance.

Maybe this is why so many of the movies in the latter half of Tarantino's career feature or center on revenge. Among other things, *Inglourious Basterds* is the story of Shosanna Dreyfus's revenge on the Nazis who killed her family. *Django Unchained* tells the story of Django Freeman's revenge on slaveholders in the antebellum South who enslaved and abused him and his wife. In *The Hateful Eight*, Major Marquis Warren exacts revenge on General Smithers for his executions of black prisoners at the Battle of Baton Rouge. In *Death Proof*, Stuntman Mike's would-be victims deliver vengeance by running him off the road and beating him to death. Even the finale of *Once Upon a Time in Hollywood*, when Cliff Booth and Rick Dalton kill Charles Manson's lackeys, can be seen as symbolic revenge for the real murder of Sharon Tate.

In Tarantino's filmography, those who deserve revenge always get their wish before the credits roll. Sometimes they are destroyed in the process, like Shosanna or Major Warren. Sometimes they get a happier ending, like The

Bride or Django. But both endings can be gratifying as long as vengeance is attained. Revenge is an intense form of closure, maybe the most intense form, so it plays to genre's strengths. It's more than just gratifying. It's retributive *justice*, a kind of healing.

Drawing on its proximity to myth and fable, Tarantino tests genre's ability to provide closure not just for people's wounds, but *historical* wounds—like Nazism, American slavery, and the Manson murders. Discussing *Django* with NPR, Tarantino said he wanted to use the Spaghetti Western genre to "give [Django] the folkloric tale [he] deserves." In this case, genre offered Tarantino a mythic frame to foreground strength and resilience, in a story of retribution and a figure of empowerment. Of course, the finale of *Django*, in which the hero dynamites a slave plantation, like the finale of *Inglourious Basterds*, in which Shosanna kills the Nazi high command, can't deliver *real* closure. Those wounds are too deep. But we've always turned to stories for the resolutions we can't find in life. And we've turned to genre for the "sudden joyous turn" that J. R. R. Tolkien once described, happy endings that give "a fleeting glimpse of Joy, Joy beyond the walls of the world, poignant as grief."

In Tarantino's filmography, we see a conversation about what genre is and can do, about what these narrative formulas have carried through time from the earliest days of human storytelling. Just like Yeats's poems, Tarantino's films reinforce, deepen, and qualify all the other films in his oeuvre. He doesn't share Yeats's broad scope, but his movies exist in a common sphere of genre, with a similar style of "manic referentiality" in which "every single gesture seems always to be marked by its own cinematic nature," so new entries comment on those that came before.

In their constant quotations, the nine films in Tarantino's current oeuvre tell a different story of cinema history than you might find in a university course or a list of the best films ever made. Tarantino's oeuvre creates its own canon, one that's strange and diverse and unafraid to dumpster dive in the "trash bin of film history." It runs a twisting route through thirties gangster movies, Blaxploitation cinema, Melville's proto–New Wave noirs, Spaghetti Westerns, Grindhouse fare, sixties screwball comedies, eighties Hong Kong actioners, Italian Poliziotteschi, Giallo horror, slasher movies, hangout movies, the Shaw Brothers Studio, Douglas Sirk, Pam Grier, De Palma, Fukasaku, Peckinpah, and *much* more. This canon pays no mind to the highbrow/lowbrow divide— if anything it favors the latter. It champions so much of what our cultural memory has forgotten, evidenced by the fact that *you can't find* a lot of these movies. Some are unrestored, others out of print. Others, the film stock having decayed, are gone forever.

Tarantino's oeuvre advocates the value of neglected movies. He proves their contribution to film language, like an etymologist tracing the origin of common words to their unremembered roots. He reminds us that it's often in the "trash bins" of culture where exciting experimentation occurs. What we snobbishly consider bad taste today might in time be seen as fundamental to the medium. In this way, Tarantino's movies also illustrate just how much cinematic memory depends on the allocation of resources. What we don't preserve will eventually vanish. What we have preserved says as much about us as it does about film, what we recognize as significance.

There are as many film histories as filmgoers. For most, it's a scattershot history, drawn by our interests and what we happen to be exposed to. In a filmmaker's work, you can find a more focused history, guiding their choices, sometimes consciously, sometimes not. After a career you can connect the dots and sketch out the constellation of their influences. With Tarantino, as with Yeats, it's *always* conscious. The choices he makes are considered before the fact, and their shape doesn't just tell you something about him, but about film itself, about genre, about narrative closure and the art of performance, about neglected films and filmmakers, about cinematic memory. Tarantino's ocuvre is as expressive as any of his movies, as any individual work of art. It *is* a work of art.

Someone mind telling that to Peter Travers?

SUPERMAN IS CLARK KENT

"Superman did not *become* Superman. Superman was *born* Superman. When Superman wakes up in the morning, he's Superman. His alter ego is Clark Kent. His outfit with the big red S, that's the blanket he was wrapped in as a baby when the Kents found him. Those are *his* clothes. What Kent wears—the glasses, the business suit—*that's* the costume. That's the costume Superman wears to blend in with us. Clark Kent is how Superman views us. And what are the characteristics of Clark Kent? He's weak. He's unsure of himself. He's a coward. Clark Kent is Superman's critique on the whole human race."

So says Bill, the eponymous villain of Quentin Tarantino's revenge epic *Kill Bill*, at the film's climax. As the previous essay makes clear, I'm a big fan of Tarantino's work. But I'm a bigger fan of Superman, a Super Fan, if you will, and as a Super Fan I'm forced to explain why I think this is the exact wrong take on the Man of Steel. Of the famous Clark Kent/Superman dichotomy, Bill suggests that Superman is the real personality and Clark Kent is the disguise. I think the opposite is true. I believe Clark is the core of the character, not the superhero, and I think the best Superman stories emphasize that, while those that neglect the Kent side tend to be flat and forgettable. Clark Kent is not the creation; Superman is. Clark Kent is not Superman. Superman is Clark Kent.

Maybe it seems trivial to devote an essay in this book to superhero identity. But anyone who's known me since junior high would be more likely to wonder why only *one* chapter of this book focuses on the Last Son of Krypton. Superman was my first obsession—before Emerson or the Lord of the Rings or cyberpunk or movies. Superman switched on the obsessive part of my mind, the part that *has* to know everything there possibly is to know about a subject, the part that stays up late to read one more chapter (or comic), the part that robs focus from schoolwork or work work to daydream about fan fiction while drawing eight million Superman Ss on every page of my chemistry notebook. All my other obsessions, a few of which are covered in this book, flow from Superman.

In an earlier chapter, I describe how Emerson's essays punctured my apathy and inspired a curiosity about reading and writing that effectively rebooted my life. I *was* apathetic in secondary school, always doing the least work necessary to satisfy my parents and teachers. But outside of school, I was enthralled by the mythological multiverse of DC Comics. At the time, those two things, academics and comics, seemed like separate worlds. One was boring and mandatory, the other fun and something I chose. But fascination is contagious. The experience is more important than its object, especially for a young mind. It's a super-power all its own, a heat vision that ignites whatever it sees, even those things that used to look boring.

Superman is not a highbrow subject, but it's a dense one. There's a lot there for a kid in his early teens to explore. We're talking about one of the most recognizable fictional characters of the last century, a global icon. It's hard to imagine anyone who would be unfamiliar with the red and yellow S symbol. Since his debut in *Action Comics* #1 on April 18, 1938, which inaugurated the superhero genre, Superman has featured in thousands of original stories—mostly in the many ongoing comics that bear his name, but also in every other possible medium: television, film, radio, theater, books, video games. All these interpretations add up to an elaborate mythos that reflects the visions of hundreds of artists, beginning with Superman's creators, Jerry Siegel and Joe Shuster. Even now, eighty-some-odd years later, that mythos continues to grow, maybe at a faster rate than ever before. For a young me, Superman was a never-ending wellspring of new adventures to devour.

For all the thousands of chapters in the Superman story, the basics of the mythos are simple and familiar. In his acclaimed series *All-Star Superman*, Grant Morrison captured the backstory in four panels and eight words:

Doomed planet.
Desperate scientists.
Last hope.
Kindly couple.

The *doomed planet* is Krypton, Superman's home world. The *desperate scientists* are his birth parents: Jor-El and Lara, who tried to warn Krypton's leaders that the planet was on the verge of exploding. The *last hope* is Kal-El (Superman's Kryptonian name), who was launched by his parents into space before the tragedy, the only survivor of his species. And the *kindly couple* is Jonathan and Martha Kent, farmers from Kansas who discovered a spaceship with a baby inside and decided to raise him as their son, Clark.

In slightly more words, the same origin is told on the first page of *Action Comics* #1 (minus the Kents, who don't appear until a year later), and these points remained more or less fixed throughout the decades.

You know what comes next:

Clark grows up in Smallville and finds that he has special physical abilities, including but not limited to invulnerability, super strength, super speed, super hearing, super breath, X-ray vision, heat vision, and flight. Influenced by the virtuous moral code of his adoptive parents, Clark decides to use his powers to help others. He moves to Metropolis and dons two costumes: the red and blue tights of Superman, and that of a mild-mannered reporter who works at the city's premier newspaper, the *Daily Planet*. At the *Planet*, he meets Lois Lane, also a reporter (and a damned good one), who falls in love with Superman but won't give Kent the time of day. At some point, Superman encounters Lex Luthor, his archnemesis, a genius threatened by the Man of Steel's power. Throw in kryptonite, a green mineral that makes Superman ill, and you've got the essentials covered.

But these are just dots on a timeline. It's the job of writers and artists to join them. What was Krypton like? Why did Jor-El send his son to Earth? What did the Kents teach young Clark? What was it like to gain such power at an early age, to be so different from your peers? How did it feel for Clark to learn about his alien heritage, the destruction of Krypton? What was the rationale for keeping his abilities a secret? Why does he feel responsible for helping human beings when he's not one? What drew Clark to journalism? What does Lois see in the Man of Steel? What made Lex so hateful and insecure? How did humanity react to the arrival of Superman? Did they immediately embrace him as the hero he claimed to be? Or were they concerned, confused, scared?

Every era of Superman tries to answer some of these questions. New writers draw from their predecessors, but also invent new details and motivations. Only the bullet points are canonical; the rest is open for interpretation. Siegel and Shuster didn't concern themselves with the interior life of Superman. After their one-page backstory, it's straight into feats of strength and derring-do, which is what their mostly young audience wanted. Later, as comics readers got older, plots and characters grew more sophisticated. We still want Superman to punch monsters, of course, but we also want a little more psychological and emotional authenticity—as much as that's possible, anyway, in a world where superheroes fight monsters for the fate of the multiverse, monthly.

In trying to achieve this authenticity, modern writers of long-running superhero titles face a common problem: the bullet points of the hero's backstory were created in an era when psychological reality wasn't important. On one hand, you have an audience that demands deeper takes on classic characters. On the other, you have narrative frameworks that didn't account for deepness, but which cannot be altered in fundamental ways (at penalty of death from fans and the hero's corporate owners). Modern writers have to work backward from iconic but hastily conceived origin stories. They have to find ways to join the dots that offer something more than feats of super strength.

This is easier for some superheroes than others. Take Batman, whose backstory we're just as familiar with: a young Bruce Wayne witnesses the murder of his parents by a petty thief in Gotham City, then vows to avenge their deaths by fighting crime. To strike fear into the hearts of criminals, "a superstitious and cowardly lot," he takes on the likeness of a bat. As with *Action Comics* #1, Batman creators Bob Kane and Bill Finger cover the origin story in nearly a single page, and the essential points haven't changed in eighty years. Despite that, Batman still resonates with modern audiences, and writers have found a number of compelling ways to enrich the psychology of the character within the boundaries of a decades-old narrative skeleton. That's because the Batman origin was psychologically and emotionally rich from the start.

At the heart of the character is *trauma*, the murder of his parents. Bruce Wayne decides to become Batman as an act of vengeance. He's a man obsessed. That obsession drives him, but it also prevents him from processing the trauma in a healthier way. Writers have mined this precarious mental state for lots of good drama. Every time Batman ventures into Gotham City's underworld, it's as if he's descending into his own tortured psyche. In his villains, we see his personal demons, never letting him rest.

Tormented antiheroes fit the modern sensibility. We like our heroes flawed and our villains sympathetic. Maybe that's because we've witnessed too much messy reality to buy pure goodness. Maybe it's because pure goodness is boring. Maybe it's because the conflict that really captivates us is not physical, but internal. When new writers tackle old heroes, we want them to ground the character's choices so they make sense to us today. But we also want to see them struggle with those choices, as we do with ours. The character of Batman lends itself to that.

What about Superman? Does the Boy Scout in blue tights, the tireless defender of Truth, Justice, and the American Way, fit the modern sensibility? Not in the way Batman does, that's for sure. We can sympathize with someone's parents being killed, but can we sympathize with someone's alien home planet exploding? We can relate to a man risking death to avenge his loved ones, but can we relate to an invincible being who protects the entire world? We can empathize with a crusader, but what about a man of steel?

I think we *can* empathize with Superman, but it's harder to pull off. In many ways, the Man of Tomorrow is a relic of values past. He's a symbol of that goodness we no longer recognize in the world. He's the epitome of the classic hero the antihero was invented to modernize. His idealism smacks of naïveté, and in the comics he's regularly mocked for this by other heroes, especially Batman.

This is why many consider Superman a boring character. He's too perfect, too powerful, too vanilla. Even his creators thought so, which is why they invented kryptonite, his Achilles' heel. As far as vulnerabilities go, kryptonite is not the most creative. It's little more than a narrative device in physical form, and a blunt one at that. If internal conflict is what makes a character interesting, kryptonite does the opposite for Superman. It *externalizes* vulnerability. It's a cheap way for weaker villains to gain an upper hand. But I can see why its inventors felt it necessary: *all* of Superman's villains are weaker than him.

To remedy this imbalance, DC Comics has tried to de-power Superman a few times throughout the years. In the early seventies, for example, Dennis O'Neil wrote an arc where Superman fights an alien doppelgänger made out of sand (???), who "permanently" depletes his powers by a third. The idea was to pit Supes against more modest foes, instead of having him constantly face cosmic threats. But fans weren't interested in a weaker Superman, so DC abandoned this new direction after a year, and restored their hero to full strength. The first issue after O'Neil left the comic begins, hilariously: "Trillions of miles out in deep galactic space . . ." Then he survives a supernova!

In 1986, John Byrne rebooted the character and pared back his powers again. He could no longer move planets. And a mere forty-megaton bomb left him unconscious for a half hour. (Supernovas were clearly out of the question.) Byrne's version lasted longer than O'Neil's, but eventually

Superman's powers crept back up. In the subsequent decades his strength has ebbed and flowed. When, for some wacky reason or other, Superman's powers vanish or decrease significantly, it's usually cited as an opportunity to "humanize" the character, which implies that Superman is always at risk of becoming unrelatable.

And he is. It's hard to get Superman right. It's hard to make any Golden Age hero relevant to a modern reader, but it's especially hard with Superman. De-powering him is one way to do it, but it's not the only way. There are terrific stories in which Supes is fully powered *and* fully relatable. And there are dull stories where he gets a bloody lip. I don't think you humanize Superman by focusing on the physical. He *is* too perfect in that respect. But just because he's perfect physically doesn't mean he's perfect in every way. Superman is not without psychological weaknesses. He's not invulnerable to emotion. This, I think, is what writers should focus on.

Bob Proehl said, "The best Superman is whichever one you were reading when you were twelve." The Superman I encountered at twelve *wasn't* Superman. My introduction to the character was through the TV series *Smallville*, about an adolescent Clark Kent. This was 2001, before the superhero film craze began in earnest. Today, the general public knows a startling amount about comics universes. My mom just asked me not to spoil a show about the Scarlet Witch! In 2001, I knew as little as most people. I was aware of Superman and Batman, of course, but none of the history, none of the lore. The whiff of that lore in *Smallville* is what piqued my interest.

In a move that Hollywood has now perfected, *Smallville* drew on a feeling of intertextuality to interest people in the show. The Superman mythos churned beneath the surface and part of the fun was seeing how they referenced it. The tag line said it all: "Every story has a beginning." We knew what the ending would be: Clark would become Superman. He started the show with just a few powers, ignorant of his alien heritage and unfamiliar with anyone called Lex Luthor or Lois Lane. So when Lex accidentally runs into Clark with his car in the series premiere and they become friends, or when he's shocked by a sudden ability to see through solid objects, we as the knowing audience get a little jolt: *his nemesis! X-ray vision!* These days, we're oversaturated with moments like this. But two decades ago, it was thrilling to a thirteen-year-old me. I needed to know more, so I started reading comics. I lost myself in the lore, and that's how I became a true Super Fan.

(That's the last time I'll use the term, promise.)

But if the intertextuality is what hooked me, it wasn't the reason I kept watching. Those little jolts are exciting, but they're not substantial, the equivalent of sugar rushes. The real substance of any good drama is character—internal conflict, relationships, events that explore what it means to be human. Now, I'm not saying *Smallville* was *The Wire* or *Breaking Bad*. As *Jeopardy!* once put it: "This WB drama about a young Clark Kent is basically *Dawson's Creek* with superpowers." (A little catty for *Jeopardy!*, no?) At its core, *Smallville* was a teen drama, and it adhered to that genre's conventions: love triangles, angst, horniness, scandal, episodes that end with someone staring longingly out of a window while the Fray's "How to Save a Life" plays into the credits. But *Smallville* was a pretty great teen drama, all things considered, at least for the early seasons.

It was also—and still is—the most character-driven take on Superman in any medium. It devoted more time to the psychology of Clark Kent than any movie or comics run. It simply had more time to do so. A good chunk of the series was devoted to Clark flexing his powers on evil or possessed "freaks of the week" (people granted special abilities from exposure to kryptonite), but *Smallville* really shined when it focused on Clark's mindset: his anxiety about being an outsider, his guilt about keeping his secret from those he loves, his fear of what might happen if people found out, his struggle to understand his role in the world, his gradual acceptance of the responsibility his power implies. In *Smallville*, Clark's life is far from perfect. He has power, but does power guarantee happiness? Super strength defeats baddies, but does it defeat anxiety? Does being invulnerable to physical harm mean you have nothing at all to fear? What about the fear of letting down those you love? What about the fear of being alone?

"What we tried to do," said *Smallville*'s creators Alfred Gough and Miles Millar, "is dramatize the emotions of Clark Kent regarding how and why he became a hero." It was an approach that humanized the character far more than any arbitrary reduction in power. It also humanized other figures in the mythos, who are just as important as Superman. It's taken for granted that Jonathan and Martha Kent are paragons of decency and good parenting, but *Smallville* showed us a kindly couple who were often in over their heads. They were raising a *superpowered alien*, after all. When their son turns to them with confusing, scary changes, they were frequently at a loss.

"Dad, what's happening to me?" Clark asks Jonathan after he wakes up floating a few feet above his bed.

"I honestly don't know," says Jonathan.

"I just wish it would stop."

"Look, Clark, I'm your father. I'm supposed to have all the answers. It kills me that I don't, but you got to have faith that we'll figure this thing out together." That's a caring thing to say, but cold comfort for Clark.

To my mind, the Kents *are* the mythos. I don't think you can properly humanize or even really understand Superman without devoting some time to their influence. The more nuanced you make them, the more nuanced Superman will seem. One of the major questions about Superman is: Why does he use his extreme power for good? Why is he so selfless, when power often has a corrupting effect? With such strength, Clark could've done anything. No one alive can check his power. So when he wants to play high school football and his father says no, why does Clark listen?

The corny answer is also the right one: love. The Kents give Clark what every child needs, human or Kryptonian. They are attentive and kindhearted, firm yet patient, affectionate and, most important, present. Their presence is the mirror image of the Waynes' absence. If Bruce becomes Batman as an act of vengeance, Clark becomes Superman as a reciprocation of the Kents' love. To love someone is to listen and empathize, to imagine another as complexly as you imagine yourself. Clark trusts that Jonathan and Martha have his best interests at heart because they've spent their lives proving it. To feel that someone really wants to understand and help you is a gift, and once you have it, you can't help but pass it on. Through his immense power, Clark reflects the Kents' love back at the world, a world they made his own.

This doesn't mean the relationship is perfect, of course. Love is never without some conflict, especially the love between parent and child. *Smallville* shows the friction, too, but that only makes the above more persuasive. A realistic portrayal of love, in which all three members of the Kent family are rounded characters, does more to ground the Superman origin than anything else. *Smallville* devotes more time to this relationship than other versions of the story, and as a result we get a subtler picture of Superman's motivations and moral center. As a TV show, *Smallville* was solid—a trailblazing series in some respects, a paint-by-numbers teen drama in others. As a new interpretation of the Superman mythos, I think it's an essential text.

With the limitations of comics and movies, you can't expect the same amount of screen or page time devoted to Clark's home life, which is why TV has some of the most "humanized" takes on the character. For this reason, I have a soft spot for the nineties series *Lois & Clark: The New Adventures of Superman*. Again, not prestige TV, but as an exploration of Lois and Clark's relationship, it's delightful. As I write this, we're only a few episodes into a new show on the CW called *Superman & Lois*, in which a married Lois and Clark return to live in Smallville with their twin sons. It's too early to tell how good the series will be, but it looks promising. They've already managed to humanize Clark more than in his three recent film appearances combined—but I'll get to them in a bit.

Just because comics have limited space doesn't mean they can't paint a nuanced portrait of Superman's psyche. As a medium of words and pictures, comics is an economical art, like poetry. A lot can be condensed into a

From: "Superman: For All Seasons" #1 © DC Comics

page. Take a look at these four panels from one of my favorite Superman comics, *Superman: For All Seasons.* Written by Jeph Loeb and drawn by Tim Sale, this four-part comic is a coming-of-age tale about Clark's departure from home in Smallville and his bumpy debut as Superman. Each installment reflects a season of the year and is told through the perspective of the people around Clark/Superman.

The first book, "Spring," sees through the eyes of Jonathan Kent as he prepares for his son to leave. The panels say so much about their relationship: Clark towers over his father, lifting a huge boulder as if it were a tennis ball, something it would've taken all afternoon and several tools for Jonathan to do in his prime. As it is, Jonathan is clearly not in his prime, but his son makes the difference irrelevant. Superman is so much stronger, so much more capable, than normal humans, that it must be hard not to feel inadequate, even unnecessary, in his presence. In the second panel, Pa Kent looks out at his farm in silence, the farm he spent a lifetime tending with his meager human strength, now fading. His son is about to leave the modest home Jonathan and his wife made for him and go out into the world (and perhaps beyond) to fulfill a grand destiny. We know the profound effect the Kents had on Clark, but in this panel, Jonathan seems to doubt it. What can a mortal man teach a god anyway? Loeb, Sale, and their team do a wonderful job conveying this sense of inadequacy and doubt, mixed with the heartache all parents feel when their child is about to flee the nest.

This Superman is anything but boring. And with the emotional groundwork laid, the action scenes hit harder.

Superman stories are always going to have a mythic flavor, but that does not mean they have to be BIG all the time. I read dozens of Superman back issues to prepare for this piece, from every decade, and in so many of them Supes is a shell of a character, bouncing from crisis to crisis, never given a moment to reflect. Soon as he solves one fate-of-the-world problem, another lands in his lap. I get it. We read superhero comics for the fireworks. But neglecting the personal makes even the biggest stakes feel empty.

Maybe the monthly titles aren't the best place to look for insightful, heartfelt stories. In the eighties and nineties, there were several Superman books running at the same time, each helmed by a different creative team but constantly crossing over. To finish a story set up in *Superman*, you'd have to buy *Adventures of Superman*, where a new writer and artist would pick up from the previous cliffhanger, tell their part, then pass it off to *Action Comics*, which would do the same—and round and round it went. For DC, it was a good strategy to force fans to buy more comics. For the making of compelling, self-contained tales, it was less than ideal. This is why you tend to find the best Superman stuff in "one-shots," stand-alone stories like *Superman: For All Seasons* that aren't burdened by the monthlies' dense and often bewildering continuity.

All the questions I posed above, the questions that exist between the bullet points of the mythos, can be answered with an eye to character. This is what the best Superman narratives have in common. *For All Seasons* tackles Clark's relationship with the Kents and fleshes out how they serve as an inspiration and refuge for him. When things get difficult for Superman, I usually find it more poignant when he retreats to the Kent farm (or to Lois Lane), rather than to the Fortress of Solitude.

But there is plenty to explore in the Fortress, too. In some versions, like *Superman: The Movie* from 1978, the Fortress houses the memories and consciousness of Jor-El, Superman's Kryptonian father. Clark's relationship with Jor-El is more fraught than his relationship with Pa Kent. Whatever else he is, Superman is an immigrant and a child of adoption. It's natural for him to wonder about his origins, as many adopted children seek out their birth parents when they come of age. For Clark—or Kal-El—the moment he learns about his heritage is also the moment he learns he can't return to it, and that his birth parents are dead. Imagine finding a video message from a deceased birth father you never met. It's a bittersweet gift. Maybe there's trauma at the heart of this character, too.

There's a touching scene in *Superman: The Movie* between Kal-El (Christopher Reeve) and Jor-El (Marlon Brando) that was cut out of the theatrical version of the film. You can see it in the Special Edition that was released in 2000. After Superman makes his first appearance in Metropolis, saving Lois Lane, stopping a few crimes, and rescuing Air Force One, he returns to the Fortress to tell Jor-El that he *enjoyed* being the hero, the cheers from the crowds of astonished onlookers.

"Do not punish yourself for your feelings of vanity," Jor-El says to his son. "Simply learn to control them. It is an affliction common to all, even on Krypton. Our destruction could've been avoided, but for the vanity of some who considered us . . . indestructible. Were it not for vanity, why, at this very moment, I could embrace you in my arms. My son." Kal-El reaches out his arms, as if to return his father's embrace, but quickly catches himself and puts his arms back down, embarrassed. Jor-El's visage fades.

Superman: The Movie isn't perfect, but it's remembered fondly for the performance of Christopher Reeve. The tag line was, "You'll believe a man can fly." But Reeve accomplished more than that: he makes you believe that Superman, the larger-than-life icon, *is a man*. He's wearing a goofy onesie of primary colors, reaching out to a hologram of his dead father in a crystal fortress, but all I see is the boy who lost his family, stranded in a faraway land among those who look at him with an almost religious awe.

Earlier in the film, Jonathan Kent dies from a heart attack when Clark is in his teens. At the funeral, he cries to his mother: "All those things I could do, all those powers, and I couldn't even save him." Later, as Jor-El's image disappears, it dawns on the viewer that Clark has lost *two* fathers, and his tremendous power only underscores his helplessness. The vulnerability in Reeve's eyes is far more humanizing than kryptonite. What if a villain tried to exploit it? Acted as mentor, earned his trust, then betrayed him at the crucial moment? No, it's just Lex Luthor again, trying to blow up the West Coast. Or Doomsday, punching Supes through empty skyscrapers, wreaking empty havoc.

My biggest gripe with the recent Superman movies— *Man of Steel*, *Batman v Superman*, and *Justice League*—is that they rarely make use of the characters' rich psychology. And what they do use is a bit puzzling. In *Man of Steel*, for example, Pa is so protective of his son's secret that he suggests Clark may have done the *wrong* thing by saving his classmates from a bus accident. Later, he refuses to let Clark rescue him from a tornado because it would betray his true self to onlookers.

This is the opposite of Jonathan's death in *Superman: The Movie*, which shows the limits of Clark's power. In *Man of Steel*, Clark *could* have saved his father but doesn't. If anything is worth revealing yourself, surely it's saving the life of your dad? What's worse, this death doesn't seem to have any psychological bearing on the CGI slugfest that comprises the final hour of the film, in which the solution to defeat the villain is . . . to snap his neck?

Listen, I'm open to new interpretations of the mythos. If it makes for a good story, I'll forgive almost anything, even a breaking of the famous rule that "Superman does not kill" (which wasn't always but is now one of those canonical bullet points). But in *Man of Steel*, it just feels lazy. So does the death of Superman in *Batman v Superman*, when he sacrifices himself by impaling Doomsday with a kryptonite spear, after another CGI slugfest. And as much as I like *Superman: The Movie*, the ending, where Superman flies around the Earth so fast he *reverses the planet's rotation and turns back time*, is pretty lazy, too, and nonsensical.

I don't think any of the live-action Superman movies is a slam dunk. Maybe the demands of blockbuster cinema are to blame. Maybe studios think people will riot if there isn't enough action, so they give audiences their money's worth. These days, that usually involves the abovementioned slugfests monopolizing the last act of the film. There's nothing wrong with a CGI fight, only a *boring* CGI fight, and pretty much all of Superman's cinematic bouts are boring. We now have the technology to present the Man of Steel's power in all its glory, but we don't seem to know what to do with it. Supes never does anything clever with his powers; he's just a blunt force object. If all he does is punch really hard, again and again and again, slugfests become snoozefests.

Hopefully, future filmmakers will figure out how to stage a Super brawl that is genuinely thrilling. But I set my hopes higher than that. I would love to see a Superman movie that doesn't rely on mass destruction for a finale. There are other ways to resolve a narrative. What about— and I'm just spitballing here—an ending that relies on wits, not strength, a finale that turns not on Superman's fists, but Lois Lane's pen? Lois and Clark are reporters, supposedly great ones, but that part of their characters is only ever paid lip service in the films. They evoke the clichés about bustling newsrooms and grumpy editors, but actual investigative reporting is absent. That's a shame, especially in the case of Lois, who always gets relegated to Superman's love interest or cheerleader or damsel in distress. The love triangle between Lois, Clark, and Superman is obviously a big part of the mythos, but Lois is so much more than a romantic object. Batman is the World's Greatest Detective, so he gets to feature in lots of great mystery stories. Why shouldn't Lois Lane, Ace Reporter for the *Daily Planet*, get to unravel some mysteries of her own?

In 2020, Greg Rucka wrote a twelve-issue comic called *Lois Lane: Enemy of the People*, which gives the character a chance to spread her investigative wings, to define herself apart from Superman. Screenwriters ought to take note. As with the Kents, the more nuanced Lois is, the more compelling the mythos becomes—including the romance.

There are things Lois can do that Superman can't. There are things Clark the reporter can do that he can't as a superhero. Superhearing and X-ray vision are useful (if probably illegal) investigative tools, but they won't make a source trust you or sharpen your prose. Superman can save the people of Metropolis from a burning building, but Clark can expose the contractors who cut costs by using cheap, flammable cladding and the city officials who lined their pockets by looking the other way. To paraphrase Lois from *Enemy of the People*, Superman can thwart the hammer of evil, but Lois and Clark can go after the arm swinging it, and the system that grants it freedom of motion.

The powers that influence the world are not always physical. In those spheres, as in the spheres of psychology and relationships, Superman is as powerful and powerless as anyone. In fact, his physical perfection makes him the *ideal* character to explore these parts of human nature. In him, the nonphysical is thrown into the starkest possible relief. A great Superman story shouldn't turn on what physical might can do, but all it can't.

Which brings me back, finally, to Bill. He seems to believe that Clark Kent is a god's interpretation of human beings: weak, unsure of himself, a coward. This, he says, is how Superman views our species. It's true that the Clark who works at the *Daily Planet*, who stumbles and stutters and can't open a soda bottle for Perry White, is partly an act.

(How else is he going to fool a room of Pulitzer winners?) But so is Superman, the icon, the symbol, the embodiment of virtue. These are dual roles.

When Clark wakes up in the morning, he's neither the symbol nor the secret identity. He's the boy who grew up in Smallville, the son of Jonathan and Martha, the friend and colleague and sometimes husband of Lois Lane, a journalist for a great metropolitan newspaper, an immigrant, a child of adoption who yearns for a family he never met, a person who accepts the responsibility his power implies, who tries to reciprocate the love he received to the world that took him in. Clark Kent is not a critique of the human race. He is part of the human race. In all the ways that matter, including and especially his weaknesses, he is human. He's one of us. As he says in *Lois & Clark*: "Superman is what I can do. Clark is who I am."

Yes, I know. I just spent six thousand words refuting one fictional character's argument about another fictional character. I should probably go outside. In Tarantino's defense, he may have written Bill's take on Superman *to be wrong*. He's the villain, after all. Wrong is what villains tend to be, especially about heroes. Bill gives his little spiel about Superman as a way to convince Beatrix Kiddo, the hero (aka The Bride), that her attempt at domestic life was always doomed to fail. "You would have worn the costume of Arlene Plimpton," Bill tells her, "but you were born Beatrix Kiddo, and every morning when you woke up you'd still be Beatrix Kiddo." At heart, he says, she's a killer. Bill sees Beatrix with a villain's lack of imagination. Too often, we make the same mistake with Clark Kent.

JERRY SEINFELD'S INTANGIBLES

Jerry Seinfeld walks into a room of advertising professionals. It's 2014. He's receiving an honorary Clio award for "pushing the boundaries of creativity and his longstanding contributions" to the field. The ad people don't know it yet, but Seinfeld is about to give one of the most biting acceptance speeches in awards show history. He opens with a few thank-yous, then:

> I love advertising because I love lying. In advertising, everything is the way you wish it was. I don't care that it won't be like that when I actually get the product being advertised—because in between seeing the commercial and owning the thing, I'm happy, and that's all I want . . . We know the product is going to stink. We know that . . . But we are happy in that moment between the commercial and the purchase, and I think spending your life trying to dupe innocent people out of hard-won

earnings to buy useless, low quality, misrepresented
items and services is an excellent use of your energy.

The last line got a hollering round of applause. I'm not exactly sure why. It may have been an involuntary nervous
response. It may be that they agreed with him: it *was* an excellent use of their energy to dupe innocent people out of
hard-won earnings. Or maybe it was just relieving to hear
someone *not* bullshit them. They work in an industry that
operates on bullshit, after all—then they're asked to swal-
low the self-important bullshit of an awards ceremony?
Maybe it was nice to hear a comedian slice through that.

Watching the speech, you can see Seinfeld revels in sat-
irizing this event and roasting its attendees. What do you
expect? This is someone who made a career of mocking the
vacuousness of everyday life. Could anything be more vac-
uous than an awards show for advertising in which he was
receiving *an honorary prize*? "This is the award they give
you when they don't think you can actually win one," he
points out. Despite that, despite its meaninglessness, Seinfeld is happy with the award in the same way he's happy
with a shoddy product "in that moment between the commercial and the purchase." It's a happiness as stupid as the
award, as the event, as advertising, and it "will last until I
get to the edge of this stage, when it hits me that this was
all a bunch of nonsense."

It's a funny speech, delivered in that signature high-
pitched lilt that makes even caustic remarks sound good-
natured. And they *are* caustic, as much of Seinfeld's comedy
is. As he's said many times, the source of all those observa-

tional bits is irritation: "If you are not easily irritated, it is hard to be funny." But Seinfeld's not irritated by his irritability. He knows it's a golden comedy goose, and if it makes normal socializing a struggle, if it strains relationships at times, you just have to take the good with the bad. "I've got a pretty good hand of cards here," he says of himself. "I'll take the bad along with it . . . It comes as a set. You don't get to pick what you want."

This is Jerry Seinfeld's characteristic point of view. You hear it in his comedy, in interviews, in the Clio acceptance speech. He's an incisive critic of society, human behavior, and himself, but most of the time his criticisms don't encourage change, but acceptance. We're used to hearing opinionated people—on Twitter, on TV, at Thanksgiving, on stand-up stages—come down on their side of an argument with righteous force. Seinfeld's opinions have force, but little righteousness, or rather he locates his righteousness in a different place than most people. Civilization is absurd and hypocritical because people are, he implies, and both will remain so forevermore. Enjoy the good, laugh at the bad. Accept that it comes as a set.

Despite his reputation as a comic who jokes about nothing, Seinfeld is often as philosophical as his "deeper" peers. It's just that his worldview is more implicit than, say, George Carlin's, who embarked on long, hilarious polemics about religion and censorship and American hypocrisy. Carlin is the forefather of a dominant mode in today's comedy: an enlightened, speaking-truth-to-power, almost journalistic style. Jon Stewart took the mantle from Carlin, then passed it down to his mentees—Stephen Colbert,

John Oliver, Trevor Noah, Samantha Bee, Hassan Min-
haj, Larry Wilmore—who went on to conquer late night
television in the US. I'm a fan of all these comics. They've
produced hours of razor-sharp material, which is hysterical
and informative, without sacrificing one for the other.

But this is not Seinfeld's lane.

He's not a "message" comic. He avoids politics and
never approaches an activistic tone. Can you imagine Seinfeld doing a bit on private prisons? I can't even imagine
him saying the words. To some extent, this apoliticism
puts him at odds with the current trend, which reflects
a renewed culture of activism in the general public. On
Last Week Tonight, John Oliver will do twenty minutes on
private prisons, and you'll come out of it with knowledge
about a topical issue, and maybe even some motivation to
push for change. You won't learn much from a Seinfeld
set—not about anything more important than Pop-Tarts,
anyway—and you definitely won't feel motivated to join
a protest or open your wallet for a cause. And that's fine.
Comedians aren't obligated to educate, or talk about "important" subjects, or provoke self-reflection. All they have
to do is make you laugh. They can achieve that by dissect-
ing political hypocrisy or sledgehammering watermelons.

Seinfeld may not be an activist, but he does turn a critical eye on our society, and what he sees there is often as
damning as anything John Oliver describes, and sometimes
more subtle. The Clio speech is a good example of this.
Seinfeld strikes at the essence of advertising, which may be
a creative and clever craft, but is exploitative at heart. Ads
pull whatever emotional strings they can to prompt a pur-

chase. They manipulate us in gross ways to generate desire, to make us feel need where it doesn't exist. And, as Seinfeld points out, much of advertising is really *false advertising*, exaggeration and truth-stretching, using glue instead of milk so a bowl of cereal will look more appealing.

In ridiculing advertising, Seinfeld indicts our warped culture of materialism, in which we're made to feel less than for not having as much crap as our neighbors and friends. Maybe "indict" is too strong a word. Seinfeld removes the gilding from a self-important event like the Clios, he helps us to see an unpleasant truth about our society, but he doesn't go further than that. Instead, he suggests that there's something to *cherish* in the perverted relationship we have with advertising: the small period of joy between the purchase and getting the crappy product.

"A brief moment of happiness is pretty good," he says. "I also think that just focusing on making money and buying stupid things is a good way of life. I believe materialism gets a bad rap . . . If your things don't make you happy, you're not getting the right things."

Obviously, Jerry's being sarcastic. But is he really? I get the sense he wants it both ways. Advertising (and by extension, capitalism) only offers us a superficial happiness, and maybe that's not the most we could hope for, but it's not bad, either. Superficial joys are still joys, after all. They're "pretty good" and pretty good is good enough.

There's something strangely freeing about this perspective. We know consumerism and materialism are Bad Things. They're words that are only ever used in a pejorative way. We know that a system that encourages the acquisition of more and more stuff (in which advertising plays an essential role) negatively affects the environment, and creates all kinds of inequities and incentives to exploit others. We know this. We know it and we decry it at every opportunity. We decry it on our $1,000 iPhones, in our new cars, at our homes decorated with all manner of junk, like that Argali rug from West Elm that really ties the room together. We are all hopelessly entangled in the system we criticize. That's a feature of global capitalism: the implication of everyone in a great number of morally messy activities. It can make you feel bewildered, impotent, guilty, apathetic—most of all, hypocritical. This constellation of feelings, this forced cognitive dissonance, is what Seinfeld excels at articulating.

In his marvelous bit on garbage, for example, Seinfeld envisions the bizarre world consumerism creates and the bizarre people it makes us into. The premise is more lucid and concise than most anti-capitalist manifestos:

> All things on Earth only exist in different stages of becoming garbage. Your home is a garbage processing center, where you buy new things, bring them into your house, and slowly crapify them over time.

All our stuff, Seinfeld says, is garbage-in-waiting, decaying even before we buy it. In some ways, this is literally true. One upshot of a booming consumer culture is the practice of *planned obsolescence*, a policy of producing goods that rapidly become obsolete and require replacing. And if our things don't become functionally obsolete, they become fashionably obsolete. We are continuously encouraged (via advertising) to get the latest and greatest, lest we be left behind. As industrial designer Brook Stevens put it, this approach should instill "in the buyer the desire to own something a little newer, a little better, a little sooner than is necessary." What does that say about the value of our things? For much of what we own, its fate as trash is a foregone conclusion, and the houses where we keep it all begin to take on a weird aspect. They begin to look like "garbage processing centers."

Seinfeld goes on to describe the journey of garbage through the processing centers we insist on calling home. Objects start on the kitchen table, "the place of honor for the new arrival," before being demoted to a cupboard, then a closet, then the garage. "No object has ever made it out of the garage and back into the house," he says. "The word *garage* seems to be a form of the word *garbage*."

You can just picture your own garage, can't you? That pile of crap that's been slowly eroding the parking space since the late nineties. As the years pass, and we get struck by this or that fleeting enthusiasm, we accumulate mountains of garbage. We can't bear to reflect on our compulsive buying habits—often a coping mechanism for deeper issues—so we hide our trash in places where we can't see it: drawers, cupboards, the basement, the garage. Seinfeld points this out without being didactic or denigrating. The critique is concealed within the laughs.

The only thing that can save our hidden garbage from the landfill, he adds, is eBay: "Why don't we mail our garbage back and forth to each other?" Now, the world is a garbage-processing center, and we're the workers who transfer the trash from one place to the next. In Seinfeld's surreal vision, humans are subordinate to their things. We do their bidding (literally). Like the best satire, it rings true, which is why we wince a little. Some of what he says is barely an exaggeration, like his description of storage units: "Now, instead of free garbage, you pay rent to visit your garbage." It *is* perverse. But that's the world of mass consumerism, which needs us to develop a ravenous love affair with stuff to perpetuate itself. By shifting the viewpoint, Seinfeld helps us see this more clearly. Again, he's not prescriptive, just descriptive, but what a description it is!

Jon Stewart once said of Seinfeld: "He is able to comedically articulate an intangible for people. When they see it they go, 'Gah! That's been in my head and I know it's been in there, but I've never put it together with that kind of rhythm, in four levels, and that's hilarious.'"

As I said in my essay about Emerson, articulation is a form of magic to me, and I'm drawn to those who can do it well. Fundamentally, there is no difference between what Seinfeld does and what Emerson does. They both articulate the world. They help us to see reality with fresh eyes. Their ends may be different—for Emerson, it's to spark reflection; for Seinfeld, laughter—but their toolbox is the same. And comedians, more than essayists and other writers, task themselves with interpreting the world from unusual angles. *Everything* is suspect to them, open to radical readings, from the most profound to the most mundane.

In his Netflix special, *Jerry Before Seinfeld*, Seinfeld talks about encountering *MAD* magazine as a kid. "You start reading it and you're going, 'Well, these people don't respect anything!' And that just exploded my head. You don't have to buy it. You could say, 'That's stupid. This [*gesturing to the world*] is stupid."

The "it" you didn't have to buy was conventional wisdom, the generally accepted assumptions that attach themselves to all we do. For comics, conventional wisdom is the enemy, and they're ruthless in pulling it apart. Sentence for sentence, minute for minute, stand-up comedians produce a greater number of revelatory experiences for people than other articulators. This is why we feel a strong connection to our favorites. Sometimes, a laugh is the recognition of what you always believed but couldn't put into words, like Stewart describes. Other times, it's shock at a startlingly true idea or point of view you never thought about before. Still other times, it's the realization that your perspective is flawed or polluted by conventional wisdom.

These are moving experiences in their own right, but they're made more so by the fact that laughing is so pleasurable. A laugh is an emotional and physical experience, which all but ensures that the big ones will stick in your memory. No disrespect to Emerson, but don't expect belly laughs from his essays. This is the advantage comedians have over other interpreters of experience: absolutely everyone is looking for a laugh, so they have the potential to reach an enormous segment of the population.

This is also their great challenge. Bits *must* be coherent. There's no wiggle room on this. If a paragraph of writing is a little confusing, you can reread it. If a joke is confusing, the joke fails. Live comedy must be perfectly intelligible to a diverse audience *the first time around*, which means that the best comics are master communicators, in addition to being funny. On both qualities, the comedy-going public is merciless. If a comedian isn't funny *and* lucid, they'll be weeded out. As Seinfeld says, "No one is more judged in civilized society than a stand-up comedian. Every 12 seconds, you're rated." Those who pass the test are rewarded with a unique and powerful bond with fans.

Seinfeld articulates intangibles through the lens of the trivial. By recounting the life cycle of a piece of garbage, he reframes our role in the consumer economy. By describing the experience of eating at a buffet, Seinfeld holds up a mirror to a society that invites overconsumption and the human psyche that can't resist it:

> Nobody would go into a restaurant, say to the waiter, "I want a yogurt parfait, spare ribs, a waffle, four cookies and an egg white omelet." People build these death row last meal wish lists. It's like a working model of all their emotional issues and personal needs.

Like shopping, eating is often a coping mechanism, and the buffet exploits that. Entering these "debauched Caligula food orgies," the veneer of self-control vanishes and our gluttonous nature is revealed. But we've normalized buffets so successfully that we don't register the absurdity.

Seinfeld registers it. So much of culture looks absurd and farcical and dumb to him. Very little of what he sees seems reasonable, but everyone's acting like it is. He's like a child looking at the irrational adult world, asking a million questions, but all the adults can say is, "That's just the way it is." Most people grow up and become those adults; Seinfeld grew up, but retained a child's inquisitiveness, and a child's impatience with the moronic and the dull.

Maybe this is why a lot of his stand-up is told from the perspective of himself as a kid. In his first special, *Stand-Up Confidential* from 1987, Seinfeld even inserts filmed skits of his childhood, seen through the lens of "comedy X-ray specs" that lets the "general public be exposed to the way comedians view our world." Seinfeld plays himself as a six-year-old, towered over by his parents and their friends, who are fitted with bodysuits to exaggerate the perspective. Young Jerry dances around but can't get the attention of the adults, who launch platitudes at one another.

The inanity of their clichés reflects the inanity Seinfeld sees throughout the adult world. As a kid, he watched his mother spend hours in the wallpaper store, flipping through giant books of patterns. "It was like the Quran," he says, mimicking her zeal. "She was looking at the patterns: '*Yes, I understand what they're saying!*'" It's a funny and relatable memory that smuggles a critique of suburban middle-class values. Mrs. Seinfeld treated wallpaper as a religion, like millions of Americans still do with their home décor. If it's not wallpaper, it's clothes or gadgets or food or cars. (It's well known that Seinfeld cherishes cars with the same reverence his mom cherished wallpaper.) On balance, these things play a larger role in our lives than traditional religion does, and have for decades. They're what we turn to for meaning and comfort and fulfillment. As a kid, Jerry could see that in his mother's eyes.

I don't think Seinfeld aims to impart Profound Critiques with his comedy. In fact, I bet he'd scoff at the suggestion. What he cares about most is laughs, and there are plenty of ways to get them that don't involve deep insights. Much of what appears to be insightful, he admits, is just "comedic sleight of hand." At a recent *New York Times* event, he said, "A lot of comedy sounds like you're driving to a point of logic or perspective, and you're really just setting up a joke. It's a technique." A good example of this is his donut hole bit, which has a philosophical feeling to it:

> A hole does not exist. Words have meanings! A hole is the absence of whatever is surrounding it. If they were really donut holes, the bag would be empty.

but is really just clever wordplay. There's no deeper meaning to this joke. It's just silly, and that's fine. Seinfeld doesn't differentiate between bits that have meaning and bits that don't. Laughs are the only vital criteria.

"I never put anything above the laugh," he told Marc Maron on his *WTF* podcast in 2020. "Self-revelation, opinion, insight, all these things—I'd never weigh those more than a laugh."

"But occasionally they intertwine," responded Maron.

"If they want to. I don't worry about that part."

The conversation between Maron and Seinfeld is illuminating. Maron spends the better part of an hour trying to understand why Seinfeld doesn't reveal more of himself in his comedy. For Maron, insight and self-revelation are vital parts of stand-up. "I got into it for the pursuit of a certain personal truth," he says. Comedy is a way to "share the truth" and "disarm big ideas that were threatening." It's "how you become who you are. It's deep, man!"

If Oliver represents "message" comedy, Maron represents what you might call "confessional" comedy, another dominant mode of the current era. Confessional comics bear their souls onstage, using the format to analyze their fears and flaws in funny ways. The forefather of this style is Richard Pryor, who spoke with remarkable candor about his drug addiction, failed marriages, experiences with racism, and more. Seinfeld called him "the Picasso of our profession." Like Picasso, Pryor changed the medium, influencing generations of artists who came after: Chris Rock, Bill Hicks, Sarah Silverman, Jerrod Carmichael, Doug Stanhope, Kevin Hart, Mike Birbiglia—the list goes on. I'm a fan of this style, too. The fearlessness of these comics, their readiness to be vulnerable, has made for some breathtaking and breathtakingly funny work. Confessional comics are not above silly laughs, but as Maron says, they use comedy to pursue emotional truth.

This is not Seinfeld's lane, either.

But that doesn't mean truth is absent from his material. I actually think Seinfeld is being a bit disingenuous when he's blasé about a joke's relationship to insight. Yes, he has some nonsensical bits, jokes built out of witty wordplay, but most of his material springs from a careful scrutiny of life. By prioritizing the laugh—the biggest laugh

from the largest number of people—he's actually prioritizing the most universal truths. That requires a lot of self-
examination, even if the jokes don't call attention to it.

"There is proper acclaim," the comedian John Mulaney
says, "given to confessional, self-revelatory, sometimes dark,
writing, performing or stand-up. But there are things people ignore in observational humor, or jokes that seem small,
where you go, 'That's that whole person right there.'"

Mulaney is a brilliant comic whom people often compare to Seinfeld. He also works in the "observational" mode,
with a little more willingness to mine his personal life for
material. "There are jokes that seem just like an innocuous,
everyday observation," he says, "that are just as dark about
human nature as any real tear-open-your-guts-and-show-
all-the-horrible-sides-of-yourself comedy."

As proof, he cites Seinfeld's bit about refusing to dis-
pose of your trash at movie theaters:

> There is an agreed-upon deal between us and the
> movie theater people, whoever the hell they are,
> and that deal is understood by every single person
> in this room. The deal is: you're ripping us off. Ok.
> We get it, we're fine with it. Lots of overpriced,
> oversized crap we shouldn't be eating to begin
> with . . . In exchange for that, when I'm done with
> something, I open my hand.

Mulaney goes on: "That line, 'I open my hand,' and the
way he says it, that's as dark and shitty as we are as human
beings. No, *you* clean it up. That is as [dark] as saying, 'I

left my wife and kids cause I'm God.' We all relate to [the feeling of] No, I'm not throwing that away."

Mulaney's right: the bit has a lot going on beneath the surface. It speaks to our selfishness, our laziness, our child-like craving for fairness and revenge. It speaks to the ease with which we dehumanize others, and the system that makes it even easier by forcing us into transactional rela-tionships. After all, it's the theater company that rips us off, that sells us the "overpriced, oversized crap we shouldn't be eating to begin with." We get even by leaving our popcorn buckets behind, but it's not the company that cleans our trash. It's the minimum wage employee, who works two jobs just to keep her kids in school.

But that doesn't stop us, does it?

Do I think Seinfeld arrived at this bit from a desire to probe the dark heart of human nature, or because he wanted to examine the transactional essence of relation-ships in late capitalist society? No. I think he got irritated when "the movie theater people" asked him to pick up after himself, then realized it's funny that most moviegoers don't think twice about leaving their trash behind, that we've all tacitly agreed it's okay to do that. Seinfeld sees a world of tacit agreements, and his hair-trigger crankiness prompts him to question them all. As Will Durant said, "we are what we repeatedly do," and what we do the most are the trivial things, the things we don't think twice about, the things our nature prompts us to do, the things society gives us tacit permission to do. The totality of Seinfeld's mate-rial, all of it composed with a poet's ear for rhythm and brevity, paints a picture of humanity that's as true as those of confessional comics, because the tedium of our lives defines us as much as our deepest fears and yearnings do.

Seinfeld sees us and judges us for our absurdity. He sees society and judges it for the same. But none of his judgments is that harsh. We *could* be better people, yes. We *could* pick up our trash after the movie, we *could* quit duping innocent people out of hard-won earnings, we *could* stop buying so much useless garbage-in-waiting, we *could* exercise a little self-restraint at the buffet, we *could* find a better religion than wallpaper, we *could* fight for a system that prioritizes people over profits and real relationships over transactional ones.

We could and we do. The man who lost control at the buffet organized a protest. The woman who left her popcorn bucket in the theater aisle opened her wallet for a cause. The mother who obsessed over wallpaper patterns raised her son with love and pride. We can always be better, but the undertow of the modern world is strong. We are constantly being dragged back into its absurdities and hypocrisies. Seinfeld, who is both critic of and apologist for humanity, doesn't want to condemn us for our mistakes and weaknesses. Plenty of others are happy to do that. Seinfeld just wants to make fun of us.

ON FRIENDSHIP

The body misleads. It's discrete, separate; its edges are well-defined. Every second of your life the distinction between "my body" and "not my body" is reinforced. You see the book in your hands and know that you are not this object. Tight as you hold it, the paper will not become a part of your body. You hug your friend. You look at her and think: *She is there, I am here.* You say goodbye and your bodies go separate ways, each its own whole.

Situated in a body with its clear-cut boundaries, your mind imagines it is equally distinct. It imagines its edges are as well defined as those of the body it controls, that it can easily tell where "I" ends and "not I" begins; that when friends part, their identities part, too, and go separate ways. The sensory experience of the body teaches us to think of ourselves as individuals, as discrete entities interacting with other discrete entities in the world.

Individuality is an intuitive concept, and being intuitive, it's also politically persuasive. This is why individualism, the social theory that prizes the moral worth of individuals, is at the heart of liberal society. As the great philosopher of liberalism, John Stuart Mill, said in 1859: "Over himself, over his own body and mind, the individual is sovereign." Societies organized around this principle protect *individual* rights, expand *individual* freedoms. Their legal systems rely on *individual* responsibility. They value *self*-reliance, promote *personal* choice, *independence*. The body trains us to think of ourselves as individuals from within. Society teaches the same from without—and misleads.

I don't want to argue with John Stuart Mill. I'm not here to say that individuality is a bogus concept. We all have a sense of self, and that sense is valid and necessary to live. It guides our actions, determines our ambitions and habits. There's no perfect answer to the question "Who am I?" but we all make an attempt. We throw whatever we can into the stew of self-concept: likes, dislikes, memories, hopes and fears, skills, job, gender, ethnicity, race, nationality, temperament, physical traits, top ten movies, favorite sports teams, how we think others view us, how we view others, how we think others view how we view others, romantic desires, work ethic, where we fit in our network of relationships. And from these ingredients emerges a unique identity, our individuality, which evolves with age and every new experience.

I don't wonder about the existence of individuality. I wonder about its boundaries, its edges. Are they as sharp as the body's? Are we as discrete as society leads us to believe? Is there a bright solid line between two people, two identities, two partners, two friends? For a long time, I've had a feeling that there isn't—that identity, "who I am," is more porous and *shared* than we commonly presume. Maybe my body isn't the outer limit of myself.

I first had this thought in Boston, at college. Elsewhere in this book I describe what an intellectually formative time that was for me, but it was also emotionally formative. If I felt detached from my education in high school, as I explain in my essay on Emerson, I also felt somewhat detached from other people. That might sound odd to those who knew me then, but it's true.

School felt to me like a social gauntlet. I wanted to be liked, but more than that, I wanted *not* to be disliked. Like millions of kids, I feared being the one who's teased, laughed at, avoided. Because I had a last name like Puschak ("poo," then "shack"), enterprising jerks had a head start, so I had to build defenses fast. My chosen shield, the one that proved the most useful, was comedy. Nothing defuses like a joke, as all class clowns know. Nothing deflects the laser beam of ridicule like a laugh. Making someone laugh is the quickest way to get them to like you, and when you're a kid, it doesn't take much. You don't have to be Seinfeld, you don't need polished bits. Silly voices, writing something childish on the blackboard, a pratfall, recycling a movie quote—any of these will do the trick. All class clowns are hacks, but they know how to get a laugh.

My school years were joyful, but when you're always playing the social game, the popularity game, you tend to keep others at a distance. The distance might not be that great, but it's enough to prevent a deeper connection. That's because trying to be "cool" is a defensive posture. You don't let people all the way in because that's what makes you vulnerable. The blasé attitude that's a signature of so many "cool" teenagers is just emotional armor. In high school, I followed a maxim best articulated by Michael Douglas in the abysmal 2009 romantic comedy *Ghosts of Girlfriends Past*: "The power of a relationship lies with whoever cares less." Like the insecure and handsome Matthew McConaughey, I had to outgrow this immature philosophy if I ever wanted a loving relationship with my childhood sweetheart, Jennifer Garner—or anyone else.

I'm still outgrowing it. Learning to lower your defenses, learning how to love and be loved, is a life's work. For me, that work began on a shitty morning in 2008:

I woke with one of those hangovers that feels fine until you stand up out of bed and the room spins like a Teacups ride that's come loose from its tracks. In twenty minutes, I had a meeting on the far side of campus with an academic advisor to discuss my application for a study abroad program in New Zealand. I ate as many Frosted Flakes as my stomach could handle (seven), drank some water, and journeyed out into a Boston so cold my back muscles seized. From my earliest days at BU, I had dreamed of traveling to New Zealand, where the school had an internship program in partnership with the University of Auckland. Now that the semester was finally approaching, I was giddy. I'd been talking about it for months, researching New Zealand, reading about internships, watching the Lord of the Rings on repeat (has there ever been a better tourism ad?). I arrived at the advisor's office with a minute to spare, managed a crooked smile through the apocalyptic headache, and was promptly informed that I failed to take a course required for my major and so did not qualify for any study abroad programs—before vomiting onto his desk.

Okay, I added the last part for dramatic effect.

I get it: woe is me! This is microscopic on the scale of actual problems, and what's worse, it was my fault! But it was a hinge point for me, one of those times when your life goes in an unexpected direction. The next semester arrived, my two closest friends left for their own study abroad programs, and I remained in town, feeling lonely, attending a profoundly boring class I should have completed a year prior. But as is often the case with shitty life moments, it turned out to be a gift in retrospect, and I owe that to new friends.

That semester I fell in with a group of people who had until then been only acquaintances, faces I'd seen in corridors, at parties. It's funny to think back on it now, after more than a decade of close friendship, after all the experiences, the late nights, after living through our twenties together, figuring out our careers, after attending (and one time, officiating at) their weddings, after holding their children. It's funny to think about those first hangs, how nervous I was, how determined not to show it. Back in freshman year, I relied on old habits to make friends: jokes and buffoonery. With this new group, I did the same but toned it down a bit—because *I* was toned down. I was twenty then, questioning my interests, values, identity. I was vulnerable and ready to lean into that feeling for the first time. I don't know if they could sense that in me. Maybe it was obvious. But they were generous all the same.

And that, of course, is the key. I say "of course," but generosity is a tough lesson to learn when you prioritize being liked. Worse than defensive, it's selfish. Your chief concern is your own feelings, while friends become a means to insecure ends. Self-absorption corrodes friendship. It corrodes all other relationships, too, but friendship is the laboratory where most of us discover that for the first time.

Family ties are imbalanced by nature, but they can survive all kinds of crap because the members are stuck with one another (in most cases). Romantic relationships usually occur later in life than friendships and draw from the lessons learned (or not learned) in them. If you can't maintain a healthy friendship, there's little chance you'll make a romantic partnership work. To quote the famous line: "friends are the family you choose." They can also choose to walk away, much easier than family can, if the relationship ceases to be rewarding. To have good friends, you have to *be* a good friend. You have to be selfless and caring and generous—all the corny things McConaughey learns in the third act of *Ghosts of Girlfriends Past*. And if you can take these things to heart before your mid to late thirties, without being guided Scrooge-like on a tour of past, present, and future toxic relationships, all the better.

This is what my new friends taught me, by example, and I did my best to reciprocate what I was given: I invested in their lives, tried to be helpful, compassionate, a good listener. I opened up, let myself be vulnerable, shared my hopes, anxieties, insecurities, told them I loved them. I felt their ups and downs as my own, and knew the reverse was true. I realized that I could be loved for who I was, not merely for the amusement I could provide. In truth, I'd been loved for who I was all along; my new friends helped me see that. They helped me to recognize and appreciate the generosity of old friends and family, which I'd been a beneficiary of for so long.

This might sound clichéd, and it definitely sounds mushy, but in this case the mushy, clichéd things are true—in the abstract, anyway. In practice, love among friends doesn't usually manifest in sentimental ways. We didn't sit in a circle and bare our souls to one another, while Norah Jones played in the background. We sat in a half circle and gaped at the increasingly ridiculous twists in the final season of *Lost*, scream-arguing about what it all meant. We got too drunk at An Tua Nua, danced like idiots, stopped one another from making bad decisions (unless we were *really* drunk, in which case we encouraged them). We championed one another's projects, lent a hand when asked, attended screenings and gallery shows and concerts. We made absurd videos together and developed a shared sense of humor. We teased, played practical jokes, took it too far, let tiny squabbles escalate into big fights, acted like jerks, forgave one another, laughed about it in retrospect. We met one another's families, visited one another's homes, vacationed in Key West, lived together in Los Angeles, ate two thousand slices of Domino's pizza in Boston, road-tripped from New York City to Portland. A friendship is made up of dozens of big moments and thousands of tiny ones: rides in the back of a cab, late-night eats, laughs about stuff no one else finds funny (or even understands).

If you've been in a tight group of friends, you know how special it can be. The bond between ten (or five or fifteen) people who know one another intimately, who love and like one another, is unlike anything else in the sphere of relationships. There's a sublime sense of unity in a close group of friends, a sense of belonging, of relaxation, of not having to put on an act. At twenty, I wasn't sure what kind of act I should be putting on anyway, so it was a gift to have that freedom. For many, college is a time of transition, a time to evaluate the person you've been, the person you created instinctively while growing up, and begin to fashion the person you want to be going forward. I felt very malleable in those years. I don't think it's a coincidence that it's also when I made my deepest friendships.

I can't speak for them, but it seemed to me like we were forging our identities together, as well as forging a shared identity. It was through them that I worked things out—sometimes explicitly, in conversation or over text; other times implicitly, through laughter and frustration, agreement and disagreement, observation and empathy. Choosing a friend is an act of identity-building. You're choosing a complement, and complementary pieces describe each other. As friends grow closer, the interplay of their identities becomes more complex, more reciprocal. Soon one of the most salient features of X's self-image is "best friend of Y," and vice versa. In a group of close friends, you're the complement of many; several identities weave into a pattern, a tapestry that is greater than the sum of its individuals.

At some point, I began to wonder: Is it possible that I am *fundamentally* entwined with my friends? Why exactly do I insist on thinking of myself as individual and separate? Is that just a trick of the senses, a false assumption rooted in my experience of the body? A cultural norm? I owe so much of my personal development to others. If you magically removed those others, these friends, from my life, who would I be? If I went back in time and took COM 201 when I was supposed to and went to Auckland, who would I be? Not me. Not this me, anyway. Some things would be the same: my temperament, my sweet tooth, my hopelessness at sports. But the parts of me I made with my friends, the parts that *are* my friends, would be gone, and they're essential. I'm used to thinking of individuals as the basic unit of humanity, but maybe it's *shared* identities that matter most.

What does science have to say about this?

On the concept of identity, the social sciences have a lot to say—too much for me to adequately cover here. It's a complex subject, but it's also a murky one; identity means different things to different fields of study (psychology, sociology, politics, etc.), even to different scholars in the same field, and the nuances are rarely clarified. This has led some to suggest that we drop the term altogether. What's funny is that we seem to have no issue using "identity" in casual conversation. It's one of those words we think we understand but would struggle to explain if pressed.

In a handy essay called "Identifying Identity: A Semantic History," Philip Gleason tries to clear up some of the ambiguity by tracing the uses of the term through time. Interestingly, you don't have to go that far back to find identity's origins, at least in the sense that we think of it today: an individual's self-conception.

This connotation emerged and became popular in the 1950s from the work of German American psychologist Erik Erikson. Before emigrating to the United States on the eve of World War II, Erikson studied with Sigmund Freud's daughter Anna in Vienna, and his work is rooted in psychoanalytic theory, Freud's id-ego-superego model of the psyche. Erikson deemphasized the sexual dynamics that obsessed Freud, focusing instead on the development of the self through eight life stages. For Erikson, this process was psycho*social* in nature.

In each stage, the person confronts a "crisis" that can be resolved positively or negatively. In the first stage, for example, from birth to eighteen months, the disoriented infant looks to the caregiver for stability. The crisis here is between *trust* and *mistrust*. If care is consistent and predictable, the baby will gain a sense of trust that carries into future relationships. If needs are not met, the opposite happens. Healthy personalities, argues Erikson, stem from positive resolutions of these crises.

Each stage strengthens what Erikson called the "ego identity." In stage four (age twelve to eighteen, adolescence), the identity becomes self-conscious, and we begin to define for ourselves who we are and what roles we'll assume in our social communities. Friends play a big part in this stage, as they're who we compare and contrast with. As Erikson describes, adolescents "help one another temporarily through much discomfort by forming cliques and by stereotyping themselves, their ideals, and their enemies." The crisis of this stage is *identity* versus *role confusion*. If adolescents fail to find a stable identity for themselves during this transitional period, they'll feel anxious and unsure, a lack of self-esteem.

Erikson coined a familiar term for this: "identity crisis."

Most of us, I'm sure, have experienced an Eriksonian identity crisis—if not in adolescence, then later in life. It describes what I went through when I failed to meet the requirements for Auckland. Of course, it wasn't really about a study abroad program. New Zealand was just an escape, a way to sustain momentum, so I didn't have to work on myself. Staying back arrested that momentum and forced me to face up to my role confusion.

At twenty, I was technically in Erikson's fifth stage, characterized by the crisis of *intimacy* versus *isolation*. "The young adult," he says, "emerging from the search for and the insistence on identity, is eager and willing to fuse his identity with that of others. He is ready for intimacy, that is, the capacity to commit himself to concrete affiliations and partnerships and to develop the ethical strength to abide by such commitments, even though they may call for significant sacrifices and compromises."

There are a lot of problems with psychoanalytic theory, but this strikes me as true to life. In my college friends, I was looking for genuine connections, not mirrors to reflect an image of myself. I was ready to make the compromises that required. Maybe this is what I felt as a shared identity: the "fusing" of intimacy Erikson describes.

Erikson laid out his stages of psychosocial development in *Childhood and Society*, published in 1950. In the years that followed, Gleason notes, the cachet of this model grew among intellectuals. "As other books followed in quick succession over the next few years, Erikson and his ideas became something of a cultural phenomenon." This is how the sense of "identity" as we know it entered the cultural drinking water, finding its way into books and classrooms and overpriced self-help seminars.

After Erikson opened the door, identity theories proliferated. Some built on his psychosocial model; others reacted against it. In almost all cases, identity is considered to have personal *and* social aspects, which are fundamental and inseparable. Where scholars differ (and this often depends on whether they're psychologists or sociologists) is on what aspect matters more. Is identity primarily created by the individual mind? Or primarily socially constructed, based on the roles we play, the groups we identify with? There is no definitive answer, and there never will be. The study of identity, like the study of the mind more generally, can't be an exact science.

But inexactness isn't uselessness. Most theories of identity contain insights that have sharpened our knowledge of this elusive concept. They've given us a structured language to test against our experiences. That language has helped me understand and articulate the bonds I have with loved ones, how my identity is dependent on theirs, and vice versa. We aren't as discrete as the body implies. Our identities *do* blend, and the intricacy of that blending in a group of friends is a unity all its own.

In day-to-day life, it's far more practical to think of and refer to ourselves as individuals. After all, that's how society thinks of us: *I* am responsible for *my* actions. If *my* boss gives *me* a job to do, my group of friends isn't responsible to complete the task as a shared identity. *We* won't shoulder the blame if the task isn't completed. *I* will. But if I'm fired, my friends will feel the pain of that firing as their own. If I'm despondent as a result, that gloominess will alter the dynamics of the group until I recover, which they'll help me to do, just as antibodies rush in to neutralize pathogens. Most of the time, it's practical to think of ourselves as individuals. But in times of love and times of need, we are never as alone as it sometimes seems.

The social sciences are important tools for understanding the links between people, but scholarly language is often excessively complex and made impenetrable with jargon. When I went looking for accurate representations of my experience, I didn't find them in textbooks or academic journals. I found them in fiction:

> And now I ask, "Who am I?" I have been talking of Bernard, Neville, Jinny, Susan, Rhoda, and Louis. Am I all of them? Am I one and distinct? . . . I cannot find any obstacle separating us. There is no division between me and them. As I talked I felt "I am you." This difference we make so much of, this identity we so feverishly cherish, was overcome.

That's Virginia Woolf, from her 1931 novel, *The Waves*. Of all the evocations of friendship I've read, this is the most powerful. Her prose is the opposite of dry; it's lush, as lyrical as fiction can get without being poetry.

Building on techniques she developed in *Mrs. Dalloway* and *To the Lighthouse*, *The Waves* tells the story of a group of six friends, from childhood to old age, through the interior monologues of each person—*only* interior monologues. There's no narrator, and we never hear the friends actually talking to one another. Imagine the show *Friends*, but all you hear are the characters' thoughts—and they're all as eloquent as Virginia Woolf.

It's a bizarre, sometimes difficult reading experience, but once you adjust to the rhythm of the text, it absorbs you. At this point in Woolf's career, she was in total command of her craft, and you can feel that control as the prose flowers and dances. Maybe it *is* poetry. Critics have described the book as a prose poem. Or maybe the distinction doesn't matter. That would fit the theme, as *The Waves* is obsessed with probing distinctions, namely, the distinctions between people. Several times in the book, the friends wonder whether they are distinguishable from one another, or if they make an indistinguishable union:

> But when we sit together, close . . . we melt into each other with phrases. We are edged with mist. We make an unsubstantial territory. (Bernard)

> How curiously one is changed by the addition, even at a distance, of a friend. How useful an office one's friends perform when they recall us. Yet how

painful to be recalled, to be mitigated, to have one's self adulterated, mixed up, become part of another. (Neville)

We have tried to accentuate differences. From the desire to be separate we have laid stress upon our faults, and what is particular to us. But there is a chain whirling round, round, in a steel-blue circle beneath. (Louis)

The common fund of experience is very deep. (Jinny)

The still mood, the disembodied mood is on us, we enjoy this momentary alleviation (it is not often that one has no anxiety) when the walls of the mind become transparent. (Rhoda)

I am not one person; I am many people; I do not know altogether who I am—Jinny, Susan, Neville, Rhoda, or Louis: or how to distinguish my life from theirs. (Bernard)

These are only a few of the reflections the characters have on this subject. Bernard thinks about it the most, almost to the point of obsession (which makes me wonder if I'm the Bernard of my friend group, zealously reading social science theory for corroboration of an eccentric intuition, while the others live their lives in peace, never thinking twice about what sort of sublime unity we form). The others don't dwell on it as much, but even when they're not thinking about the group's interdependence, they betray it in other ways:

> What then is the knowledge that Jinny has as she dances; the assurance that Susan has as, stooping quietly beneath the lamplight, she draws the white cotton through the eye of her needle? They say, Yes; they say, No; they bring their fists down with a bang on the table. But I doubt; I tremble.

The friends are constantly sizing one another up, as Rhoda does with Jinny and Susan here, then measuring themselves against what they see—or think they see. The assessments are very often flawed, which we learn once the POV shifts to the person in question. What seems like assurance is actually disguised anxiety. What seems like a sense of self-reliance is actually a feeling of intense isolation. This, too, strikes me as true to life. The things we see in our friends are not always there. The observations say as much about us as them. But this only contributes to the union of the group. We observe, we project, we react, we reflect, we adjust. Even flawed judgments feed into the mix. Sometimes we become what we think others think we are. Other times, we rebel against what we think they think. Either way, we're affected.

In healthy friendships, these dynamics are talked through. I tell my friend who I think I am, and she listens. She does the same. She describes what she sees in me, and I listen. I do the same. As a result, we observe and judge each other with nuance, and feel comfortable in that mutual patience and tolerance, in that love. Maybe that ideal is never fully achieved—we are too imperfect for that—but the best friendships get pretty close.

In the unconventional style of *The Waves*, we glimpse Woolf's own point of view. Though there is plenty of individuality in the content of each friend's inner monologue, the prose, as critic Carl Woodring says, "imposes a single undifferentiated style on the consciousness of all six." The poetic, exuberant language flows from one mind to the next without break. From that river emerges, by turns, Bernard, Rhoda, Jinny, Neville, Susan, and Louis, but the emphasis is as much on the river itself as the souls that comprise it. It's not only that I see a true portrait of friendship in this novel; I *feel* it in Woolf's rhythm. Social science theory can't match this for verisimilitude, which might be unfair because other novelists can't match it, either.

Maybe it's unnecessary to invoke science and fiction to justify my feelings about friendship. Maybe I ought to trust that my experience has value in itself. I *know* the individuality we feel is only part of the story. I *know* this sense of separateness is an accident of biology and culture. I *know* that "I" am only part of "me," and that the rest is comprised of others, my family, my friends. As John Donne wrote, "No man is an island, entire of itself"—but there I go, quoting again. It's hard not to, when minds like Erikson and Woolf and Donne offer their remarkable powers of articulation to your situation. In a sense, they are part of me, too, just as you are, just as this essay, this book, is a part of both of us. I write it, but I don't make it. We make it together. It is, to invoke Woolf a final time, "the healthy offspring of a close and equal alliance between us." It is a token of the places where we're not separated.

Recently I've been thinking a lot about my friends from college. I met them at a bend in my life, a period when "I" was unsettled, and together we created something in which I discovered myself, my shared self. I'm writing this at what I fear is another bend. I'm thirty-three. Almost all of us are married now, a few have children. We've scattered to different cities to pursue careers or be near family or explore the world. For years, people older than I am have warned that *this* is when friendships begin to fade, as people make families of their own. Always I brushed this off, believing it would not, could not, happen to us. We would always be as close as we were in Boston. Now I know we'll probably never be that close again.

If you're my age or older, maybe you know what I mean. It's not that we love one another less; it's that there's no substitute for physical proximity and the free time of early adulthood. Priorities shift, responsibilities grow, we make choices. I'm as big a culprit as any. I keep moving to new cities, unable to settle. I see photos of my friends' kids, and they look so old, and I realize how much I've missed. I no longer share in all the biggest developments of their lives. Sending a text, making a call, video-chatting, double-tapping an Instagram post—it's not the same, is it?

Is this how it happens? Not with a bang, but with gaps between hangs that gradually get larger, and you forget to send that birthday message, and you're surprised to learn they actually left that job six months ago, and "Where are

you living these days?" and the only time you all get together is at weddings, but the weddings are running out,
then months turn into years into decades and you're telling
optimistic thirtysomethings that *this* is when friendships
begin to fade. Please do not let me be that guy.

I'm not resigning us to that fate, not yet. I'm old enough
now to know that it's possible to grow distant from your
closest friends. But it's not a foregone conclusion. These
people mean too much to me. These people *are* me. The de-
stabilizing feeling that sinks my stomach at the thought of
losing them proves that better than any model of identity,
better even than the brilliance of Virginia Woolf.

So I'll work to stay in their lives. I'll make an effort to
see them. I'll listen and share, ask for advice, tell them I
love them. The distance between us makes it harder, but it's
only our bodies that are distant.

And the body misleads.

WRITE A BOOK

The first day was bad. The second was worse. On the fifth, I began cursing myself out loud. On the sixth, I began doing it in public. Know how you can be so consumed with a line of thinking you forget you're walking down Harrison Street to pick up Tito's Burritos? On the sixth day, in the early evening, I was muttering "stupid fucking stupid" to myself at a crosswalk in Southwest Portland, waving my forefinger in figure eights. Twenty minutes later I said "because you're dumb" in an elevator with two people who thankfully did not live on my floor. On the seventh day, the last day of the first week, I gave up. It was the fourteenth or fifteenth time I'd done so. Giving up started to feel insincere, which was a welcome development. Not as welcome as writing a single sentence that didn't make me wince and/or doubt the value of my entire life, but welcome nonetheless. So I embarked on my second week with hope. It was a bad week.

It wasn't until week five of writing my novel that I had a good day. By then I had discovered a few things: that I was a poor writer, and not just a poor writer but a worthless person, and not just a worthless person but a despicable one. I discovered these things several times every day, always in that order. My work rang false, I learned, because I had nothing to say, and I had nothing to say because I had little interest in actually writing, only in being a writer. I wanted to be a writer because I was vain, attention-starved, and at the core of me was a black hole where a soul ought to be. Anyway, on my first good day I wrote two not entirely terrible paragraphs. One of them contained this sentence:

He began his sojourn to that blistery junction of tri-district gambling not six months before, dreaming of a streak, but all he got was a dark new appreciation for settling debts.

I don't know what could make a junction blistery, but in December 2010 I thought it sounded perfect for my science fiction novel about an ecumenopolis, or a planet-wide city. Remembering how harshly I judged myself back then, it's a wonder so many of these lousy sentences made it into the final draft. For every sentence that survived, at least twenty were discarded in a spasm of self-loathing. God knows what horrors lurk in earlier drafts if "blistery junction" made the cut.

So much of that book seems dreadful to me now—I was twenty-two, so maybe that's to be expected—but it didn't seem that way on my first good day. After weeks of punching myself in the heart, a morning in which I looked back over my work and felt satisfied was deeply relieving. The cruel autobiography playing on loop in my head became a little less persuasive. I slept soundly and woke with optimism, ready to capitalize on this change in momentum . . . only to fall by lunch into a vortex of even crueler cruelties than before. That was one of those days when you're so filled with disgust that getting out of the house doesn't seem drastic enough so you spend most of the afternoon looking at flights you'll never take to cities in Europe and Asia. In those early months, I did a lot of research on Zen monasteries in Japan, mentally bracketing the next five years for a severe regimen of silence and self-abnegation. The only remedy for my monstrous personality was, obviously, "successful transcendence of ego consciousness and a quasi-mystical embodiment of pure, incorporeal Buddha-nature."

In the end I never went to Japan, but I did have donuts.

The bad days after my first good day were just as bad as the ones before it, often much worse, but they were different. The bad days before my first good day were shattering. The ones that came after felt less like a wildfire inside my identity and more like a losing spin on a slot machine that basically never pays out. Both can be demoralizing, but the former is threatening in a way the latter isn't. A good day had occurred, and it was not ludicrous to imagine that a good day might occur again. But how many bad days and good donuts would I have to endure until it did?

Just five, it turned out—days.

Midway through my sixth week I had another good day, on which I wrote this doozy:

She dreams of the murder that never happened there, of the finely felt passion, darker than coals, that never called out to the silver moon in yearning—what a rose-thorn envy she feels for murderers! (What does this even mean?)

I may have been producing Frankenstein sentences like that, but twenty-two-year-old me approved. Good days gave me confidence to persevere, to push through the sludge of bad ones. Soon I had one good day a week. I sat at my desk each morning with a cup of coffee, praying it would be the one. More often than not it wasn't, much more often. But good days kept coming, and eventually, my relationship to bad days permanently changed.

Writing a book helped me to recognize the perpetual cycling of mood, to see it as something always in motion. Maybe that's obvious, but writing gave me the chance to observe it in real time. For the most part, I think, we try not to pay attention to the mood we're in. If it's a good mood, we're rarely aware of it. Happiness isn't introspective. It points outward, to the work or the people or the entertainment at hand. The moment I realize I'm happy is usually when the feeling begins to retreat—like air-conditioning programmed to turn on when the house gets too hot. Bad moods, on the other hand, are mercilessly introspective. They plunge inward with great speed to the most fundamental self-criticisms. As a result, I often seek out things to distract myself, like three to eleven episodes of *Parks and Recreation*.

"Life is a train of moods like a string of beads and as we pass through them they prove to be many-colored lenses, which paint the world their own hue, and each shows us only what lies in its own focus." That's not from my sci-fi novel (as if there were any doubt). It's Emerson again. I read his essay "Experience" in college and thought the quote was eloquent, but it wasn't until writing *Big City* that my own "train of moods" became visible to me. Knowing something is different from internalizing it. I knew the world was mediated by the "many-colored lenses" of my moods and temperament, but writing that book forced me to *watch* my own mind, for better or worse.

(Usually worse.)

Try it: Write that novel, that memoir you've been dreaming about. Assign yourself a daily word count. Let's say five hundred words a day. Grab a coffee, some snacks, and commit to staying put until that goal is reached. Resist distraction. Leave your phone in another room.

Now . . . write!

Quiet, isn't it? Too quiet. Better check Twitt—*stop it.*

Sit in the silence. Stare at the blank page, the white page. Bright white. Can't be good for your eyes to look at that color for long. I think there's a writing app that optimizes the screen for your eyes and—*stop it!*

Try to focus. I know it's hard to focus these days with so much content competing for your attention. Social media companies design their interfaces to be addicting because our attention's their product. It's incredible how much data these companies collect on each of us. Our privacy slips away each time we sign on to Facebook or TikTok, but of course we don't do anything about it because—*for god's sake, get a grip on yourself!*

Once you push the daydreams from your thoughts, you can usually manage six or seven sentences before the real dark stuff starts to gnaw. There's that famous quote by Ira Glass about beginners: "For the first couple years you make stuff, it's just not that good. It's trying to be good, it has potential, but it's not. But your taste, the thing that got you into the game, is still killer. And your taste is why your work disappoints you." I could not agree more. When you start as a writer, your work sucks. And, as Glass says, "it is only by going through a volume of work that you will close the gap" between your writing and your taste.

But he leaves out one very important thing: overcoming your deficiencies as a writer is going to put you in direct conflict with a part of your mind determined to see you fail. In other words, closing the gap between your skill and your taste isn't just a matter of writing a million words, but writing them while battling a relentless antagonist, one who knows your deepest secrets and insecurities. This adversary will use the crap that you're producing as a sledgehammer to split the foundations of your self-esteem. It was waiting for some hard evidence. Now you've given the enemy all the documentation it needs to prove you're a dumbass. And it *will* prove it to you, again and again, every time you sit down to write. When you commit to staying at that desk, you're committing to this psychological fight.

Self-hatred derailed me frequently. Many days I didn't reach my five hundred words, choosing instead pizza and YouTube. You can only take so much. But as with anything you do over and over, these internal clashes eventually became routine. I became familiar with the moves my antagonist would make, and though that didn't always stop the blows from landing, it did fortify me. After a while the predictability of the experience provided a certain detachment, and I was able to witness the negativity from a safe emotional distance—a perspective on a perspective.

Good days offered yet another perspective. And the frequency of them increased. Near the end of my second month, I started having two good days a week. It felt like an embarrassment of riches. Soon enough, I internalized the reliability of good days. More important, I internalized the reliability of a change in mood, from good to bad and back to good again.

The longer I worked, the more good days I had, but the scale never tipped; at best I had an equal number of good days to bad. Will it ever improve beyond that? Maybe, but I doubt it. To work on something you believe in, I think, is to expose yourself to the spectrum of your mind, to the shadows and the light.

As Seinfeld says, "It comes as a set."

After six months I finished the first draft of *Big City*. I didn't think it was the next *Gatsby* or even the next *Fifty Shades of Grey*, but completing a long-form story was incredibly rewarding. A year later I wrote a second book that was twice as long and, I thought, twice as good. (It wasn't.) My plan was to self-publish both novels by building an audience on YouTube, after seeing the success John Green achieved thanks in part to his online fan base.

I failed to realize two things, however:

First, that John was a skilled novelist who had been honing his craft for many years and I was only at the very *very* beginning of that journey; and second, that I would fall in love with the creative medium of online video. After

ten or fifteen videos, YouTube stopped being a means to
an end and became the craft I wanted to master. A decade
of making The Nerdwriter has taught me how much work
you *really* have to do, how many words you *really* have to
write, to begin to close that gap between your taste and
ability. I still have a long way to go, but I'm proud of the
progress I've made.

My early books may be crap, but writing them had an
immense impact. Learning the dynamics of my mood enabled every success I've had in work and life. When I feel
good, I exploit the feeling for all it's worth. When I feel
like shit, I batten down the hatches and hold on to my
confidence that it will pass. That's so important because it
keeps me from changing course during a bad spell, from
being tossed in the winds of my attitude. If every bad day
resulted in a deconstruction of values and priorities, I'd
never make headway on a worthwhile project.

A big undertaking, whether it's writing a novel, starting
a business, or nurturing a relationship, requires emotional
stability. But our emotions *aren't* stable, so the best we can
do is cultivate a bird's-eye view on ourselves to remind us
of the colored lens we're seeing through. Eventually the
reflex to that view becomes automatic, and that's especially
helpful when I'm at my lowest, about to trash my progress,
or make a decision I'll regret, or succumb to the gloom in
my head. With all the poise I can muster, I wait for the
clouds to pass—there are more bad hours than bad days—
and pick up the thread again.

This semblance of stability is good enough. It works.
There's nothing more important in creative work than

being able to pick up where you left off. Somewhere in my head there's a graveyard of promising ideas with tombstones that all read: "Left off on Month-Day-Year, before obsessing about something unproductive for three days and forgetting that it ever existed. RIP."

I've come a long way from that depressing evening on Harrison Street, but not that long, apparently: for some reason, I thought I'd be able to write this short essay with ease. But the 2,475 words you just read (and the 283 to come) took the better part of six weeks to complete. At least five times I exited my office crestfallen and announced to my wife that I was a poor writer, and not just a poor writer but a worthless person, and not just a worthless person but a despicable one. I was frustrated with my inability to make progress *while writing an essay about why it's so hard to make progress*. I couldn't see the lessons I was literally writing down in front of my face. That's how narrow the tunnel vision of mood can be.

But eventually the fever broke as it always breaks, as some part of me knows it will. Good days came and went. I got to work. I finished it.

ACKNOWLEDGMENTS

Thanks to my wife, Lissette, who sustained me during the writing of this book. Without her, it wouldn't exist—nor would most of the good things in my life. Thank you to my parents, Nick and Shelley, whom I owe *so* much. Sorry for all the times I was a brat. Thanks to the Bydney for being the best sister on Earth.

Thank you to my editor, Stephanie Hitchcock, for giving this book the focus it needed, for your enthusiasm, and for introducing me to the world of publishing with kindness and professionalism. Thanks to my agent, Kirby Kim, who asked me over two years ago if I had any interest in writing a book (I did), and then shepherded it through every stage of its creation. Thank you to Danielle Mazzella di Bosco for the gorgeous cover. Thanks to Sarah Weichel and Ale Catanese, for helping Kirby bring this project to life. And thanks to Nate Ruff, for always doing what's in my best interest and encouraging me to do the same.

Gràcies a Barcelona per acollir-me mentre escrivia

aquest llibre. Thanks to my local SandwiChez, where approximately 37 percent of this book was written, while listening to Brian Eno and Harold Budd's *Ambient 2: The Plateaux of Mirror.* Thanks to our friends here, who've been overwhelmingly caring. And thank you to *all* my friends. There's little I can add to the earlier essay, except to say I think about you every day, and I love you.

Finally, thanks to *you*, the readers, and everyone who's watched The Nerdwriter in the last decade—especially my Patreon patrons. In more ways than one, this book is the product of your incredible support.

WORKS CITED BY CHAPTER

A note on organization: Works are cited in the order they are referenced in the text, not alphabetically; however, for several sources within one master source, such as essays from a single volume, the essays are gathered into a single entry, in order of reference, rather than separately.

EMERSON'S MAGIC

Ralph Waldo Emerson. *Journals of Ralph Waldo Emerson*. Boston: Houghton Mifflin Company, 1909.

———. "Nature," "The American Scholar," "The Divinity School Address," "Self-Reliance," "Montaigne; Or, The Skeptic," "Experience," and "The Poet." In *The Complete Works of Ralph Waldo Emerson*. New York: Wm. H. Wise, 1926.

John Haynes Holmes. "The Enduring Significance of Emerson's Divinity School Address." Harvard Square Library. 1938. www.harvardsquarelibrary.org/cambridge-harvard/enduring-significance-divinity-school-address/.

John Townsend Trowbridge. "Reminiscences of Walt Whitman." *Atlantic Monthly* 89 (February 1902): 163–175. https://whitmanarchive.org/criticism/interviews/transcriptions/med.00570.html.

I THINK THE INTERNET WANTS TO BE MY MIND

Mark Kaufman. "The Devious Fossil Fuel Propaganda We All Use." *Mashable*, July 13, 2020. www.mashable.com/feature/carbon -footprint-pr-campaign-sham/?europe=true.

BP (@bp_plc). "The first step to reducing your emissions is to know where you stand. find out your #carbonfootprint with our new calculator & share your pledge today!" Twitter, October 22, 2019, 4:08 p.m. https://twitter.com/bp_plc/status/1186645440621531136.

Michael Roberts, host. "Tim Cook on Health and Fitness." *Outside* (podcast). December 9, 2020. https://www.outsideonline.com /podcast/tim-cook-health-fitness-podcast.

Facebook. "Third Quarter Report for 2020." Facebook, n.d. http:// d18rn0p25nwr6d.cloudfront.net/CIK-0001326801/518957aa -c936-455b-8ba0-9743ca4c3855.pdf.

"Zuckerberg Says He Doesn't Want Facebook to Be Addictive." Bloomberg Technology, November 20, 2020. www.youtube .com/watch?v=DmdCZ_ArQ2w.

Rahmatullah Haand and Zhao Shuwang. "The Relationship Between Social Media Addiction and Depression: A Quantitative Study Among University Students in Khost, Afghanistan." *International Journal of Adolescence and Youth* 25, no. 1 (2020): 780–86. www .tandfonline.com/doi/full/10.1080/02673843.2020.1741407.

Betul Keles, Niall McCrae, and Annmarie Grealish. "A Systematic Review: The Influence of Social Media on Depression, Anxiety and Psychological Distress in Adolescents." *International Journal of Adolescence and Youth* 25, no. 1 (2020): 79–93. www .tandfonline.com/doi/full/10.1080/02673843.2019.1590851.

Yubo Hou, Dan Xiong, Tonglin Jiang, Lily Song, and Qi Wang. "Social Media Addiction: Its Impact, Mediation, and Intervention." *Cyberpsychology: Journal of Psychosocial Research on Cyberspace* 13, no. 1 (2019), Article 4. https://doi.org/10.5817/CP2019-1-4.

Anna Vannucci, Kaitlin M. Flannery, and Christine McCauley Ohannessian. "Social Media Use and Anxiety in Emerging Adults."

Journal of Affective Disorders 207 (2017): 163–66. https://doi
.org/10.1016/j.jad.2016.08.040.

River Donaghey. "Our Three Wishes Are All for Will Smith's Genie
in 'Aladdin' to Go Away." *Vice*, February 11, 2019. www.vice
.com/en/article/wjmxqy/will-smith-genie-alladin-trailer-deep
ly-disturbing-please-god-no-vgtrn.

Jeff Fowler (@fowltown). "Thank you for the support. And the criticism. The message is loud and clear . . . you aren't happy with the
design & you want changes. It's going to happen. Everyone at
Paramount & Sega are fully committed to making this character the BEST he can be . . . #sonicmovie #gottafixfast." Twitter,
May 2, 2019, 11:00 p.m. https://twitter.com/fowltown/status
/1124056098925944832?lang=en.

Louis Virtel (@louisvirtel). "I don't know why you're all freaking out
over miniature yet huge cats with human celebrity faces and
sexy breasts performing a demented dream ballet for kids."
Twitter. July 18, 2019, 11:55 p.m. https://twitter.com/louisvirtel
/status/1151973898168102912?lang=en.

Emily Dixon. "The 'Cats' Trailer Is Here and It's Horrifying
the Internet." CNN, July 19, 2019. https://edition.cnn
.com/2019/07/19/movies/cats-trailer-reaction-scli-intl/index
.html.

Isaac Feldberg. "'Cats' Trailer Unites Internet in Abject Terror."
Boston Globe, July 19, 2019. www.bostonglobe.com/lifestyle
/names/2019/07/19/cats-trailer-unites-internet-abject-terror
/sRio4ln6CktH98Yv2hOXzJ/story.html.

Brendan Morrow. "Downright Nightmarish *Cats* Trailer Stuns Critics: 'My Eyes Are Bleeding.'" *The Week*, July 19, 2019. https://
theweek.com/speedreads/853785/downright-nightmarish-cats
-trailer-stuns-critics-eyes-are-bleeding.

Britt Hayes. "Your Eyeballs Are Not Ready for the Horrors Within
the *Cats* Trailer." *A.V. Club*, July 19, 2019. www.avclub
.com/your-eyeballs-are-not-ready-for-the-horrors-within
-the-1836421619.

Sophie Gilbert. "I Watched the *Cats* Trailer, and I Have Some Questions." *The Atlantic*, July 19, 2019. www.theatlantic.com/entertainment/archive/2019/07/cats-trailer-questions/594367/.

Ehis Osifo. "Here Are the Funniest Tweets About the New *Cats* Trailer." *BuzzFeed*, July 18, 2019. www.buzzfeed.com/ehisosifo1/cats-trailer-reactions-twitter-tweets-jokes-funny.

Ashlie D. Stevens. "Why Do the Cats in 'Cats' Look Like Medieval Art Gone Wrong? And Other Burning Questions." *Salon*, July 19, 2019. www.salon.com/2019/07/19/why-do-the-cats-in-cats-look-like-medieval-art-gone-wrong-and-other-burning-questions/.

R. Eric Thomas. "The Five Stages of Dealing with the 'Cats' Trailer." *Elle*, July 18, 2019. www.elle.com/culture/movies-tv/a28440010/cats-trailer-why-god/.

Brian Barrett. "A Feline Anatomy Expert Weighs In on That *Cats* Trailer." *Wired*, July 18, 2019. www.wired.com/story/cats-trailer-feline-anatomy-expert/.

Ian Abramson (@ianabramson). "I put the song from Us onto the Cats trailer and I think it fits better." Twitter, July 19, 2019, 12:05 p.m. https://twitter.com/ianabramson/status/1151977667207372800?lang=en.

David Mack. "The 'Cats' Trailer Has Made the Internet Lose Its Damn Mind and Now There's Remixes." *BuzzFeed News*, July 19, 2019. www.buzzfeednews.com/article/davidmack/cats-movie-remix-trailer-music-us.

William Hughes. "This *Cats/Us* Trailer Mashup Is Hideously Purrfect." *A.V. Club*, July 18, 2019. www.avclub.com/this-cats-us-trailer-mash-up-is-hideously-purrfect-1836509960.

Lindsay Dodgson. "Someone Put the Creepy Music from 'Us' over the New 'Cats' Trailer and People Think It's Much More Fitting." *Insider*, July 19, 2019. www.insider.com/people-turning-cats-movie-trailer-into-horror-2019-7.

Jordan Peele (@jordanpeele). "Yes." Twitter, July 19, 2019, 4:13 a.m. https://twitter.com/JordanPeele/status/1152038669647114240.

Rachel Yang. "Jordan Peele Agrees: *Cats* Trailer Fits Better with the Song from *Us*." *Entertainment Weekly*, July 19, 2019. https://ew.com/trailers/2019/07/19/jordan-peele-agrees-cats-trailer-fits-better-with-song-from-us/.

Marissa Martinelli. "The *Cats* Trailer Looks Great, You Weirdos." *Slate*, July 18, 2019. www.slate.com/culture/2019/07/cat-musical-movie-trailer-fur-jennifer-hudson-memory.html.

Maura Johnston. "The 'Cats' Trailer Is Uncanny Valley Until Jennifer Hudson Sings. And Then You Realize It Could Work." NBCNews.com, July 19, 2019. www.nbcnews.com/think/opinion/cats-trailer-uncanny-valley-until-jennifer-hudson-sings-then-you-ncna1031746.

Scott Mendelson. "'Cats': With a Purrfectly Bonkers Trailer, Universal Has No Claws for Alarm." *Forbes*, July 18, 2019. www.forbes.com/sites/scottmendelson/2019/07/18/cats-taylor-swift-idris-elba-jennifer-hudson-star-wars-jumanji-greatest-showman-la-la-land-trailer-box-office/.

Mike Snider. "Netflix's Biggest Competition? Sleep, CEO Says." *USA Today*, April 18, 2017. www.usatoday.com/story/tech/talkingtech/2017/04/18/netflixs-biggest-competition-sleep-ceo-says/100585788/.

Emily Gaudette. "Netflix Just Declared a War on Sleep." *Newsweek*, November 17, 2017. www.newsweek.com/netflix-binge-watch-sleep-deprivation-703029.

Liah Greenfeld. *Mind, Modernity, Madness: The Impact of Culture on Human Experience*. Cambridge: Harvard University Press, 2013.

THE COMFORTS OF CYBERPUNK

Chris Eggertsen. "'Altered Carbon': Inside the Drama's 15-Year Road to Netflix." *The Hollywood Reporter*, February 1, 2018. www.hollywoodreporter.com/tv/tv-news/altered-carbon-inside-dramas-15-year-road-netflix-1080944/.

Matt Dolloff. "*Blade Runner 2049*'s Estimated Budget Revealed." *ScreenRant*, September 15, 2017. https://screenrant.com/blade -runner-2049-estimated-budget/.

Mariella Moon. "CD Projekt Red Made Hundreds of Millions on 'Cyberpunk 2077' Despite the Refunds." *Engadget*, April 23, 2021. www.engadget.com/cd-projekt-red-cyberpunk-2077-2020 -fiscal-year-earnings-040643067.html?guccounter=1.

Janez Steble. "New Wave in Science Fiction or the Explosion of the Genre." Doctoral dissertation, University of Ljubljana, 2004.

J. G. Ballard. "Which Way to Inner Space?" May 1962. *New Worlds Science Fiction* 40, no. 118 (May 1962).

Rob Latham. "From Outer to Inner Space: New Wave Science Fiction and the Singularity." *Science Fiction Studies* 39, no. 1 (2012): 28–39. https://doi.org/10.5621/sciefictstud.39.1.0028.

William Gibson. *Neuromancer*. New York: Ace Science Fiction Books, 1984.

Bruce Sterling. *Mirrorshades: The Cyberpunk Anthology*. New York: Arbor House, 1986.

———. Preface to *Burning Chrome*, by William Gibson. New York: Ace Books, 1987.

Lance Loud. "*Blade Runner*." *Video Verité*. www.videoverite.tv/pages /llwritingbladerunner.html.

Larry McCaffery and William Gibson. "An Interview with William Gibson." *Mississippi Review* 16, no. 2/3 (1988): 217–36. www .jstor.org/stable/20134176.

William S. Burroughs. *Naked Lunch*. New York: Grove Press, 1959.

William Gibson. *Count Zero*. New York: Arbor House, 1986.

———. Interviewed by David Wallace-Wells. "William Gibson: The Art of Fiction No. 211." *Paris Review* 197 (Summer 2011). www.theparisreview.org/interviews/6089/the-art-of-fic tion-no-211-william-gibson.

Frederick M. Dolan. "The Poetics of Postmodern Subversion: The Politics of Writing in William S. Burroughs's *The Western Lands*." *Contemporary Literature* 32, no. 4 (1991). https://doi.org/10.2307/1208515.

Ridley Scott, director. *Blade Runner*. Warner Bros., 1982.

Charles Baudelaire. *Paris Spleen*, trans. Louise Varèse. New York: New Directions Publishing Corporation, 1970.

———. *The Painter of Modern Life, and Other Essays*. London: Phaidon, 1964.

Georg Simmel. "The Metropolis and Mental Life." In *The Sociology of Georg Simmel*, ed. K. H. Wolff. New York: Free Press, 1950.

David Scribner. "Noir Romantic." *Harvard Magazine*, November–December 2010. www.harvardmagazine.com/sites/default/files/pdf/2010/11-pdfs/1110-24.pdf.

Donna J. Haraway. "A Cyborg Manifesto: Science, Technology, and Socialist-Feminism in the Late Twentieth Century." In *Simians, Cyborgs, and Women: The Reinvention of Nature*, 149–81. New York: Routledge, 1991.

GameCentral. "Cyberpunk 2077 Gamescom 2019 interview—'We Paint a Picture and We Let the Player Interpret It." *Metro*, August 23, 2019. https://metro.co.uk/2019/08/23/cyberpunk-2077-gamescom-2019-interview-paint-picture-let-player-interpret-10618408/.

WHEN EXPERTS DISAGREE

Joe Perota, director. *Last Week Tonight with John Oliver*. Season 1, Episode 3. "Climate Change Debate." Aired May 11, 2014, on HBO. www.youtube.com/watch?v=cjuGCJJUGsg&t=2s.

John Cook, Dana Nuccitelli, Sarah A. Green et al. "Quantifying the Consensus on Anthropogenic Global Warming in the Scientific Literature." *Environmental Research Letters* 8, no. 2 (May 15, 2013). https://iopscience.iop.org/article/10.1088/1748-9326/8/2/024024.

Wikipedia. "Institute of Physics." https://en.wikipedia.org/wiki/Institute_of_Physics. Last modified October 9, 2021, 19:30.

Web of Science Group. *2019 Journal Citation Reports*. Clarivate An-
    alytics, June 20, 2019. https://clarivate.com/webofsciencegroup
    /wp-content/uploads/sites/2/dlm_uploads/2019/08/JCR
    _Full_Journal_list140619.pdf.

Richard S. J. Tol. "Comment on 'Quantifying the Consensus on An-
    thropogenic Global Warming in the Scientific Literature." *En-
    vironmental Research Letters* 11, no. 4 (April 13, 2016). https://
    iopscience.iop.org/article/10.1088/1748-9326/11/4/048001.

Dana Nuccitelli. "Climate Contrarians Accidentally Confirm the
    97% Global Warming Consensus." *The Guardian*, June 5, 2014.
    https://www.theguardian.com/environment/climate-consensus
    -97-per-cent/2014/jun/05/contrarians-accidentally-confirm
    -global-warming-consensus.

James Lawrence Powell. "The Consensus on Anthropogenic Global
    Warming." *Skeptical Inquirer* 39, no. 6 (November/December
    2015). https://skepticalinquirer.org/2015/11/the-consensus-on
    -anthropogenic-global-warming/.

Andy Skuce. "James Powell Is Wrong About the 99.99% AGW Con-
    sensus." Critical Angle, April 4, 2016. https://critical-angle
    .net/2016/04/04/james-powell-is-wrong-about-the-99-99
    -agw-consensus/.

K. Hayhoe, J. Edmonds, R. E. Kopp et al. "Climate Models, Scenarios,
    and Projections." In *Climate Science Special Report: Fourth National
    Climate Assessment*, vol. 1 (2017): 133–60. https://doi.org/10.7930
    /J0WH2N54; and B. DeAngelo, J. Edmonds, D. W. Fahey, and B.
    M. Sanderson. "Perspectives on Climate Change Mitigation." In
    Climate Science Special Report: Fourth National Climate Assessment,
    vol. 1 (2017): 393–410. https://doi.org/10.7930/J0M32SZG.

Brady Dennis, Steven Mufson, and Scott Clement. "Americans In-
    creasingly See Climate Change as a Crisis, Poll Shows."
    Washington Post, September 13, 2019. www.washingtonpost
    .com/climate-environment/americans-increasingly-see-climate
    -change-as-a-crisis-poll-shows/2019/09/12/74234db0-cd2a
    -11e9-87fa-8501a456c003_story.html.

Washington Post. "Where Democrats Stand: Do You Support Raising the Federal Minimum Wage to $15 Per Hour Nation-
wide?" *Washington Post,* November 16, 2019. www.washington
post.com/graphics/politics/policy-2020/economic-inequality
/minimum-wage/.

Leslie Davis and Hannah Hartig. "Two-Thirds of Americans Favor Raising Federal Minimum Wage to $15 an Hour." Pew Research Center,
July 30, 2019. www.pewresearch.org/fact-tank/2019/07/30/two
-thirds-of-americans-favor-raising-federal-minimum-wage
-to-15-an-hour/#:~:text=Two%2Dthirds%20of%20Ameri
cans%20(67,Center%20survey%20conducted%20this%20spring.

AllSides. "Vox." AllSides, n.d. www.allsides.com/news-source/vox
-news-media-bias.

Ad Fontes Media. "Vox Bias and Reliability." Ad Fontes Media, n.d.
www.adfontesmedia.com/vox-bias-and-reliability/.

Dylan Matthews. "The Debate About the Minimum Wage, Explained." *Vox,* November 20, 2019. Updated on January 22,
2021, and retitled "Will Biden's $15 Minimum Wage Cost
Jobs? The Evidence, Explained." www.vox.com/future-perfect
/2019/11/20/20952151/should-minimum-wage-be-raised.

Arindrajit Dube. "Impacts of Minimum Wages: Review of the International Evidence." Report prepared for the government of the
United Kingdom, November 2019. https://assets.publishing
.service.gov.uk/government/uploads/system/uploads/attach
ment_data/file/844350/impacts_of_minimum_wages_review
_of_the_international_evidence_Arindrajit_Dube_web.pdf.

———. "Minimum Wages and the Distribution of Family Incomes."
American Economic Journal: Applied Economics 41, no. 4 (2019): 268–
304. https://www.aeaweb.org/articles?id=10.1257/app.20170085.

US Bureau of Labor Statistics. "Occupational Employment and Wages
in San Francisco–Oakland–Hayward—May 2020." May 2020.
www.bls.gov/regions/west/news-release/occupationalemploy
mentandwages_sanfrancisco.htm.

———. "May 2020 State Occupational Employment and Wage

Estimates: Alabama." US Bureau of Labor Statistics, May 2020. www.bls.gov/oes/2020/may/oes_al.htm.

Arindrajit Dube. "Proposal 13: Designing Thoughtful Minimum Wage Policy at the State and Local Levels." Brookings Institution, June 19, 2014. www.brookings.edu/wp-content/uploads/2016/06/state_local_minimum_wage_policy_dube.pdf.

Michael Reich. "Likely Effects of a $15 Federal Minimum Wage by 2024." Center on Wage and Employment Dynamics, February 7, 2019. www.congress.gov/116/meeting/house/108844/witnesses/HHRG-116-ED00-Wstate-ReichM-20190207.pdf.

David Neumark. "Employment Effects of Minimum Wages." *IZA World of Labor*, 2018. https://wol.iza.org/articles/employment-effects-of-minimum-wages/long.

David Neumark and William Wascher. "Minimum Wages and Employment." IZA Discussion Paper No. 2570, January 2007. https://ssrn.com/abstract=961374.

David Neumark, JM Ian Salas, and William Wascher. "More on Recent Evidence on the Effects of Minimum Wages in the United States." *IZA Journal of Labor Policy* 3 (2014), article no. 24. https://doi.org/10.1186/2193-9004-3-24.

Eric Lipton. "Fight over Minimum Wage Illustrates Web of Industry Ties." *New York Times*, February 9, 2014. www.nytimes.com/2014/02/10/us/politics/fight-over-minimum-wage-illustrates-web-of-industry-ties.html.

ESCAPE INTO MEANING

Albert Camus. *The Myth of Sisyphus, and Other Essays*. London: H. Hamilton, 1965.

J. R. R. Tolkien. *The Return of the King: Being the Third Part of the Lord of the Rings*. Boston: Houghton Mifflin, 1965.

Ross Johnson. "The Lawsuit of the Rings." *New York Times*, June 27, 2005.

J. R. R. Tolkien. "A Secret Vice." Tolkien Online Reader, 1931. http://fac ulty.smu.edu/bwheeler/tolkien/online_reader/T-ASecretVice.pdf.

———. *The Letters of J.R.R. Tolkien*, ed. Christopher Tolkien and Humphrey Carpenter. Boston: Houghton Mifflin, 1981.

———. "On Fairy-Stories" (1939). Cool Calvary, n.d. https://coolcal vary.files.wordpress.com/2018/10/on-fairy-stories1.pdf.

"Holy (adj.)." Online Etymology Dictionary, 2020. www.etymonline .com/word/holy.

Rudolf Otto. *The Idea of the Holy*. London: Oxford University Press, 1923.

C. S. Lewis. "The Numinous." In *The Problem of Pain*. New York: Macmillan, 1962.

Michael Pollan. *How to Change Your Mind: What the New Science of Psychedelics Teaches Us About Consciousness, Dying, Addiction, Depression, and Transcendence*. New York: Penguin Press, 2018.

Chris Brawley. *Nature and the Numinous in Mythopoeic Fantasy Literature*. Jefferson, NC: McFarland, 2014.

Tom Grater. "Alan Moore Gives Rare Interview: 'Watchmen' Creator Talks New Project 'The Show,' How Superhero Movies Have 'Blighted Culture' & Why He Wants Nothing to Do with Comics." *Deadline*, October 9, 2020. deadline.com/2020/10 /alan-moore-rare-interview-watchmen-creator-the-show -superhero-movies-blighted-culture-1234594526/.

ODE TO PUBLIC BENCHES

Mary Dellenbaugh-Losse. "What Makes Urban Commons Different from Other Commons?" Urban Policy, June 25, 2020. https://urban-policy.com/2017/09/18/what-makes-urban -commons-different/.

Charles Baudelaire. *The Painter of Modern Life, and Other Essays*. London: Phaidon, 1964.

Honoré de Balzac. *The Physiology of Marriage*. New York: Liveright Publishing Corporation, 1943.

Ralph Waldo Emerson. "Nature." In *The Complete Works of Ralph Waldo Emerson*. New York: Wm. H. Wise, 1926.

Samuel Beckett. *Stories and Texts for Nothing*. New York: Grove Press, 1967.

"A Prescription for Better Health: Go Alfresco." Mind and Mood, Harvard Health Publishing, October 12, 2010. www.health .harvard.edu/newsletter_article/a-prescription-for-better -health-go-alfresco.

Hon K. Yuen and Gavin R. Jenkins. "Factors Associated with Changes in Subjective Well-Being Immediately After Urban Park Visit." *International Journal of Environmental Health Research* 30, no. 2 (2020): 134–45. https://doi.org/10.1080/09603123.2019.1577 368.

Herbert Langford Warren, ed., *Vitruvius, the Ten Books on Architecture* (Cambridge: Harvard University Press, 1914).

Radhika Bynon and Clare Rishbeth. "Manifesto for the Good Bench." Young Foundation, 2015. https://youngfoundation .org/wp-content/uploads/2015/11/The-Bench-Project_single -pages.pdf.

William Hollingsworth Whyte. *The Social Life of Small Urban Spaces*. Washington, D.C.: Conservation Foundation, 1980.

Clare Cooper Marcus and Carolyn Francis, eds. *People Places: Design Guidelines for Urban Open Space*, 2nd ed. New York: Van Nostrand Reinhold, 1998.

Jan Gehl, trans. Jo Koch. *Life Between Buildings: Using Public Space*. Washington, D.C.: Island Press, 2011.

David Roberts. "Barcelona's Radical Plan to Take Back Streets from Cars." *Vox*, April 9, 2019; updated May 26, 2019. www.vox .com/energy-and-environment/2019/4/9/18300797/barcelona -spain-superblocks-urban-plan.

Marta Bausells. "Story of Cities #13: Barcelona's Unloved Planner Invents Science of 'Urbanisation.'" *The Guardian*, April 1, 2016. www.theguardian.com/cities/2016/apr/01/story-cities-13-ei xample-barcelona-ildefons-cerda-planner-urbanisation.

David Roberts. "Barcelona Is Pushing Out Cars and Putting In Superblocks. Here Are the 2 Biggest Challenges Ahead." *Vox*, April 10, 2019. www.vox.com/energy-and-environment/2019/4/10/18273895 /traffic-barcelona-superblocks-gentrification.

Justin McGuirk. "Urban Commons Have Radical Potential—It's Not Just About Community Gardens." *The Guardian*, June 15, 2015. www.theguardian.com/cities/2015/jun/15/urban-common -radical-community-gardens.

Winnie Hu. "'Hostile Architecture': How Public Spaces Keep the Public Out." *New York Times*, November 8, 2019. www.nytimes .com/2019/11/08/nyregion/hostile-architecture-nyc.html.

Amy Crawford. "Cities Take Both Sides in the 'War on Sitting.'" Bloomberg CityLab, October 20, 2017. www.bloomberg.com /news/articles/2017-10-20/cities-can-t-decide-whether-to-of fer-you-a-seat.

Sophie Davies. "COVID-19 Pandemic Puts Barcelona Urban Green- ing Plan in the Fast Lane." Reuters, January 11, 2021. www .reuters.com/article/us-spain-coronavirus-city-environment -fe/covid-19-pandemic-puts-barcelona-urban-greening-plan -in-the-fast-lane-idUSKBN29G0I2.

Ajuntament de Barcelona. "Cap a la Superilla Barcelona." Ajuntament de Barcelona, November 11, 2020. https://ajuntament.barce lona.cat/premsa/wp-content/uploads/2020/11/201111-DOS SIER-Superilla-BarcelonaVDEF.pdf.

THINKING IN OEUVRES

"Quentin Tarantino on Why He Will Quit Making Movies." *Pop- corn with Peter Travers*, December 23, 2015. https://youtu.be /mVYy49s4p-8.

"Quentin Tarantino Will Only Make Ten Films." *The Hollywood Re- porter*, December 10, 2015. www.youtube.com/watch?v=Wf nNeM3VwOw.

"See Full Interview with 'Once Upon a Time in Hollywood' Cast on TODAY." *Today*, NBC, July 15, 2019. http://youtu.be/nPom HS-gZEk.

"Quentin Tarantino on New Movie with Leonardo DiCaprio, Brad Pitt & Margot Robbie." *Jimmy Kimmel Live*, ABC, July 23, 2019. http://youtu.be/UC9huiaI7fg.

"Tarantino Talks Hateful Eight, Oscars." *ABC News* (Australia), January 19, 2016. http://youtu.be/lNzESz7pMBk.

"Special Interview with Quentin Tarantino for OK About 'Once Upon a Time . . . In Hollywood.'" Одноклассники, August 12, 2019. http://youtu.be/Ec5em1mqJtQ.

John Unterecker. *A Reader's Guide to William Butler Yeats*. New York: Noonday Press, 1959.

W. B. Yeats. "If I Were Four and Twenty." In *Explorations*. London: Macmillan, 1960.

———. "The Second Coming." In *Michael Robartes and the Dancer*. Churchtown, Ireland: Cuala Press, 1920.

Yeats Vision. "The Cycles of History." YeatsVision.com, n.d. www.yeatsvision.com/History.html.

W. B. Yeats. "Two Songs from a Play," "Sailing to Byzantium," "The Tower," and "Meditations in Time of Civil War." In *The Tower*. London: Macmillan, 1928.

Neil Mann. "A Vision (1925) A Review Essay." In *The Living Stream: Essays in Memory of A. Norman Jeffares*. Cambridge: Open Book Publishers, 2013. http://books.openedition.org/obp/1733.

George Watson. "Yeats's View of History: 'The Contemplation of Ruin.'" *Maynooth Review/Revieú Mhá Nuad* 2, no. 2 (1976). www.jstor.org/stable/20556890.

David A. Ross. "Two Songs from a Play." In *Critical Companion to William Butler Yeats: A Literary Reference to His Life and Work*. New York: Facts On File, 2009.

W. B. Yeats. "Vacillation." In *The Winding Stair and Other Poems*. London: Macmillan, 1933.

W. B. Yeats. "The Circus Animals' Desertion." In *Last Poems and Two Plays*. Churchtown, Ireland: Cuala Press, 1939.

Ella Taylor. "Quentin Tarantino: The Inglourious Basterds Interview." *Village Voice*, August 18, 2009. www.villagevoice.com /2009/08/18/quentin-tarantino-the-inglourious-basterds -interview/.

Gavin Smith and Quentin Tarantino. "Quentin Tarantino." *Film Comment* 30, no. 4 (1994). www.jstor.org/stable/43456459.

Eyal Peretz. "4. What Is a Cinema of Jewish Vengeance? Tarantino's Inglourious Basterds." *The Off-Screen: An Investigation of the Cinematic Frame*. Redwood City, CA: Stanford University Press, 2017, 200–210. www.academia.edu/14944020/What _is_a_Cinema_of_Jewish_Vengeance_Tarantinos_Inglorious _Basterds.

"BREAKING: Quentin Tarantino Loves Rom-Coms." *Late Show with Stephen Colbert*, CBS, December 16, 2015. www.youtube .com/watch?v=5JRQr4E8zkU.

"Quentin Tarantino on 'Reservoir Dogs.'" QuentinTarantinoHD, August 28, 2018. https://youtu.be/EUg-kvq1ERg.

Carol Clover. *Men, Women, and Chain Saws: Gender in the Modern Horror Film*. Princeton, NJ: Princeton University Press, 1992.

Joyce Carol Oates. "The King of Weird." *New York Review of Books*, October 31, 1996. www.nybooks.com/articles/1996/10/31/the -king-of-weird/.

Jean Ma. "Circuitous Action: Revenge Cinema." *Criticism* 57, no. 1 (2015): 47–70. www.jstor.org/stable/10.13110/criticism.57.1.0047.

Terry Gross and Quentin Tarantino. "Quentin Tarantino, 'Unchained' and Unruly." NPR, January 2, 2013. www.npr.org /2013/01/02/168200139/quentin-tarantino-unchained-and -unruly.

J. R. R. Tolkien, "On Fairy-Stories" (1939). Cool Calvary, n.d. https:// coolcalvary.files.wordpress.com/2018/10/on-fairy-stories1 .pdf.

SUPERMAN IS CLARK KENT

Quentin Tarantino, director. *Kill Bill Vol. 2*. Miramax Films, 2004.

Grant Morrison. "All-Star Superman #1." DC Comics, 2006.

Meg Downey. "The Weird and Wonderful History of Kryptonite." DC Comics, April 13, 2018. www.dccomics.com/blog/2018/04/05/the-weird-and-wonderful-history-of-kryptonite.

Dennis O'Neil. "Superman #223–#242." *Superman*. DC Comics, 1971.

Cary Bates. "Superman #243." *Superman*. DC Comics, 1971.

John Byrne. "The Man of Steel #1–#6." *The Man of Steel*. DC Comics, 1986.

Bob Proehl. "Last Sons of Krypton: The John Byrne Reboot, Part Two." *Medium*, February 13, 2018. https://bobproehl.medium.com/last-sons-of-krypton-the-john-byrne-reboot-part-two-7673ef88782d.

Jeopardy Questions. "This WB Drama About a Young Clark Kent Is Basically Dawson's Creek with Superpowers." Jeopardyquestions.com, n.d. www.jeopardyquestions.com/this-wb-drama-about-a-young-clark-kent-is-basically-dawsons-creek-with-superpowers.

Alfred Gough and Miles Millar. "Interview with Alfred Gough and Miles Millar." *Crimespree Magazine*, April 30, 2019. www.crimespreemag.com/interview-with-alfred-gough-and-miles-millar/.

Alfred Gough and Miles Millar, writers. *Smallville*. Season 1, episode 2, "Smallville/Metamorphosis." Aired October 23, 2001, on The CW.

Jeph Loeb and Tim Sale. "Book One: Spring." *Superman: For All Seasons*. DC Comics, 1998.

Richard Donner, director. *Superman: The Movie* (Special Edition). Warner Bros., 2000.

Greg Rucka. *Lois Lane: Enemy of the People*. DC Comics, 2020.

Lois & Clark: The New Adventures of Superman. Season 2, episode 18, "Tempus Fugitive." Aired March 26, 1995, on ABC.

JERRY SEINFELD'S INTANGIBLES

Jerry Seinfeld. "Jerry Seinfeld's Clio Acceptance Speech." YouTube, uploaded by Affan Khokhar on October 2, 2014. www.youtube .com/watch?v=uHWX4pG0FNY.

Tim Ferriss, host. "Jerry Seinfeld—A Comedy Legend's Systems, Routines, and Methods for Success (#485)." *The Tim Ferriss Show*, December 8, 2020. https://tim.blog/2020/12/08/jerry-seinfeld/.

Jerry Seinfeld. "Jerry Seinfeld on His Fans." *CBS Sunday Morning*, May 31, 2015. www.youtube.com/watch?v=s45JT_-7v24&t=103s.

John Oliver. "Prison: Last Week Tonight with John Oliver (HBO)." *Last Week Tonight*, July 21, 2014. www.youtube.com/watch?v =_Pz3syET3DY.

Jerry Seinfeld. "Jerry Seinfeld Stand-Up." *The Tonight Show Starring Jimmy Fallon*, December 24, 2014. https://youtu.be/HfYzlSN HapA.

Glenn Adamson. *Industrial Strength Design: How Brooks Stevens Shaped Your World*. Cambridge: MIT Press, 2003.

Jon Stewart. "Jon Stewart Interview by Rachel Maddow." YouTube, uploaded by "Jon Stewart!" on May 28, 2016. www.youtube .com/watch?v=ApRiu9DkJzk&t=1745s.

Michael Bonfiglio, director. *Jerry Before Seinfeld*. Netflix, 2017.

John Moffitt, director. *Talking Funny*. HBO, 2011.

Jerry Seinfeld. "Jerry Seinfeld Does His Best Tight Five." *The Late Show with Stephen Colbert*, January 7, 2017. https://youtu .be/984VkHzXl8w.

Jerry Seinfeld. *Is This Anything?* New York: Simon & Schuster, 2020.

Bruce Gowers, dir. *Jerry Seinfeld: Stand-Up Confidential*. HBO, 1987.

Jerry Seinfeld, "TimesTalks: Jerry Seinfeld and Colin Quinn." New York Times Events, December 2, 2016. https://youtu.be/VY ab6lODtfQ.

Marc Maron, host. "Episode 1129—Jerry Seinfeld." *WTF with Marc Maron* (podcast), June 8, 2020. www.wtfpod.com/podcast/epi sode-1129-jerry-seinfeld.

Allison Samuels. "1940–2005: Richard Pryor." *Newsweek*, March 13, 2010. www.newsweek.com/1940-2005-richard-pryor-114071.

John Mulaney. "John Mulaney Reveals the True Darkness Behind Seinfeld." *Theoffcamerashow*, May 18, 2018. https://youtu.be /u9rfr6qeYmU.

Will Durant. *The Story of Philosophy: The Lives and Opinions of the Great Philosophers of the Western World.* New York: Simon & Schuster, 1961.

Jerry Seinfeld. "Jerry Seinfeld Standup at Letterman, February 14th, 2013." YouTube, uploaded by Papá Olvidado on February 17, 2013. www.youtube.com/watch?v=UMmYRUGd9is.

ON FRIENDSHIP

John Stuart Mill. *On Liberty; Representative Government; the Subjection of Women: Three Essays.* Oxfordshire: Oxford University Press, 1974.

Mark Waters, director. *Ghosts of Girlfriends Past.* Warner Bros., 2009.

Rogers Brubaker and Frederick Cooper. "Beyond 'Identity.'" *Theory and Society* 29 (2000): 1–47. https://www.jstor.org/stable /3108478.

Philip Gleason. "Identifying Identity: A Semantic History." *Journal of American History* 69, no. 4 (1983): 910–31. www.jstor.org /stable/1901196.

Erik Erikson. *Childhood and Society.* New York: Norton, 1950.

Virginia Woolf. *The Waves.* London: Published by Leonard and Virginia Woolf at the Hogarth Press, 1933.

Laurie F. Leach. "'The Difficult Business of Intimacy': Friendship and Writing in Virginia Woolf's 'The Waves.'" *South Central Review* 7, no. 4 (1990): 53–66. www.jstor.org/stable/3189094.

John Donne. "Meditation XVII." In *The Works of John Donne*, Vol. 3, ed. Henry Alford, 574–75. London: John W. Parker, 1839.

Virginia Woolf. "Mr. Bennett and Mrs. Brown." *Collected Essays*, ed. Leonard Woolf. London: Hogarth, 1966.

WRITE A BOOK

William F. Williams. "Zen." *Encyclopedia of Pseudoscience: From Alien Abductions to Zone Therapy*. Oxfordshire: Routledge, 2013.

Ralph Waldo Emerson. "Experience." In *The Complete Works of Ralph Waldo Emerson*. New York: Wm. H. Wise, 1926.

Ira Glass. "Ira Glass on Storytelling." *This American Life*, August 18, 2009. www.thisamericanlife.org/extras/ira-glass-on-storytelling.

ABOUT THE AUTHOR

Evan Puschak grew up in the Philadelphia suburbs, then attended Boston University, where he earned a BA in film production. In 2011, he created The Nerdwriter, a YouTube series about art and culture, which he still produces, and which currently has 3 million subscribers. In 2015, Evan met his future wife, Lissette, in San Francisco, which was the best thing that ever happened to him. The two of them currently live in Barcelona, where he wrote this book.